CELIAC DISEASE
AND GLUTEN SENSITIVITY

By Michelle Denton

LUCENT
PRESS

Published in 2019 by
Lucent Press, an Imprint of Greenhaven Publishing, LLC
353 3rd Avenue
Suite 255
New York, NY 10010

Designer: Deanna Paternostro
Editor: Jennifer Lombardo

Cataloging-in-Publication Data

Names: Denton, Michelle.
Title: Celiac disease and gluten sensitivity / Michelle Denton.
Description: New York : Lucent Press, 2019. | Series: Diseases and disorders | Includes glossary and index.
Identifiers: ISBN 9781534563759 (pbk.) | ISBN 9781534563735 (library bound) | ISBN 9781534563742 (ebook)
Subjects: LCSH: Celiac disease–Juvenile literature. | Gluten–Health aspects–Juvenile literature.
Classification: LCC RC862.C44 D46 2019 | DDC 616.3'99–dc23

Printed in the United States of America

CPSIA compliance information: Batch #BS18KL: For further information contact Greenhaven Publishing LLC, New York, New York at 1-844-317-7404.

Please visit our website, www.greenhavenpublishing.com. For a free color catalog of all our high-quality books, call toll free 1-844-317-7404 or fax 1-844-317-7405.

CONTENTS

Illness is an unfortunate part of life, and it is one that is often misunderstood. Thanks to advances in science and technology, people have been aware for many years that diseases such as the flu, pneumonia, and chicken pox are caused by viruses and bacteria. These diseases all cause physical symptoms that people can see and understand, and many people have dealt with these diseases themselves. However, sometimes diseases that were previously unknown in most of the world turn into epidemics and spread across the globe. Without an awareness of the method by which these diseases are spread—through the air, through human waste or fluids, through sexual contact, or by some other method—people cannot take the proper precautions to prevent further contamination. Panic often accompanies epidemics as a result of this lack of knowledge.

Knowledge is power in the case of mental disorders, as well. Mental disorders are just as common as physical disorders, but due to a lack of awareness among the general public, they are often stigmatized. Scientists have studied them for years and have found that they are generally caused by hormonal imbalances in the brain, but they have not yet determined with certainty what causes those imbalances or how to fix them. Because even mild mental illness is stigmatized in Western society, many people prefer not to talk about it.

Chronic pain disorders are also not well understood—even by researchers—and do not yet have foolproof treatments. People who have a mental disorder or a disease or disorder that causes them to feel chronic pain can be the target of uninformed opinions. People who do not have these disorders sometimes struggle to understand how difficult it can be to deal with the symptoms. These disorders are often termed "invisible illnesses" because no one can see the symptoms; this leads many people to doubt that they exist or are serious problems. Additionally, people who have an undiagnosed disorder may understand that they are experiencing the world in a different way than their peers, but they have no one to turn to for answers.

Misinformation about all kinds of ailments is often spread through personal anecdotes, social media, and even news sources. This series aims to present accurate information about both physical and mental conditions so young adults will have a better understanding of them. Each volume discusses the symptoms of a particular disease or disorder, ways it is currently being treated, and the research that is being done to understand it further. Advice for people who may be suffering from a disorder is included, as well as information for their loved ones about how best to support them.

With fully cited quotes, a list of recommended books and websites for further research, and informational charts, this series provides young adults with a factual introduction to common illnesses. By learning more about these ailments, they will be better able to prevent the spread of contagious diseases, show compassion to people who are dealing with invisible illnesses, and take charge of their own health.

A PAIN IN THE GUT

As a young girl, Jaclyn enjoyed going to summer camp every year. She got to see friends and spend her time doing crafts and playing outside—everything a kid loves to do. One year, however, the food from the kitchen began to disagree with her, giving her intense stomachaches and causing her to lose weight. She came home from camp miserable, but the reason for her illness remained a mystery. Looking back on the following autumn, Jaclyn vividly remembered how crippling her new illness was:

> The pain became unbearable, like someone taking a knife and twisting it back and forth every time I decided I was hungry. As the stomachaches got worse, so did my mood and my exhaustion. I would spend days straight on the couch, not able to move or go to school due to the pain. My dad took me to the pediatrician, who told me it was a stomach virus that would pass. We felt a moment of relief hoping that maybe I would lay off of junk food and stick to water, vitamins, and Pepto-Bismol for a week or two. We waited a while but, unfortunately, a virus was not the case.[1]

Jaclyn was eventually diagnosed with celiac disease, a gluten-related autoimmune disease. Whenever she ate something that contained gluten, such as pasta or bread, her immune system would attack her digestive system, damaging her intestines and making it harder for her to absorb nutrients from food. After switching to a gluten-free diet, Jaclyn's stomachaches finally went away, and she was able to gain back the 50 pounds she had lost. Although there is no cure for her disease, she can live a happy and healthy life with just one dietary change.

For some people, pain such as Jaclyn's can be an ongoing, everyday struggle. Living with celiac disease or any kind of gluten sensitivity is difficult in the modern world because so much of the food people buy contains gluten, even when they would not expect it to. The undiagnosed often suffer for years without knowing what is causing their stomach cramps or bloating, and it is still

Gluten sensitivity causes intense pain and can mimic the symptoms of a stomach virus.

very common for someone to be misdiagnosed at least once before a doctor finds the real problem. Thankfully, with knowledge about celiac disease spreading, more people are being diagnosed more quickly. The process can still take a long time, however, which makes education about gluten-related diseases a priority not only in the scientific and medical communities, but for the general public as well.

The Problem with Gluten

Gluten is a mixture of proteins found primarily in wheat, rye, barley, and hybrid grains such as triticale, which is a mix of wheat and rye. Gluten gets its name from the Latin word for "glue" due to its ability to hold these grains together. At their most basic, grains such as these are made up of starch and gluten, and gluten is primarily made of storage proteins called prolamins and glutelins. These proteins carry nutrients that nourish plant embryos as they develop—a process called germination—but they are also stretchy and sticky. Gluten, as a "glue," gives foods of all kinds the structure to maintain their shape at a molecular level by forming a three-dimensional framework that can bend and stretch without breaking easily. People have gluten to thank for the flexible, chewy texture of wheat products such as bread, baked goods, and pasta, as well as for the thick, gooey texture of many soups and sauces. It is also an important part of the process that makes bread dough rise.

For most people, avoiding gluten is unnecessary. Despite the growth of the gluten-free diet as a fad, gluten is not a health risk to people who are not sensitive to it. Like low-carb diets or going vegetarian or vegan, a gluten-free diet might help with weight loss or improving mood, but it is no more

Gluten is found in many different kinds of grain and plays an important role in the creation of bread.

or less healthy than a simple, well-rounded, healthy diet. "The diet is usually harmless to try," said Adda Bjarnadottir, a nutritionist from Iceland. "There is no nutrient in gluten grains that you can't get from other foods. Just make sure to choose healthy foods. A gluten-free label does not automatically mean that a food is healthy. Gluten-free junk food is still junk food."[2]

Gluten has become more of a problem over the past few decades because it has become harder and harder to get away from. The processed food industries lean on wheat flour to give food a pleasing texture, but that means people are eating more gluten than they think. A great deal of what the average American eats has excess gluten in it, including things in which glutenous grains are not generally main ingredients. French fries, lunch meats, candy bars, salad dressings, meat substitutes, and even sometimes scrambled eggs served in restaurants hide gluten, and the list goes on. In moderation, gluten is not bad for humans to eat if they do not have a sensitivity to it, but it can be very harmful for those with celiac disease.

Fresh fruits and vegetables, which are part of any healthy diet, are naturally gluten free, but canned produce may contain gluten.

Celiac Disease and Other Issues

Although gluten is often a major part of the average person's diet, some people are born unable to eat it without harming themselves. Celiac disease is a genetic autoimmune disorder triggered by the consumption of gluten, and studies predict that 1 in 133 Americans, or less than 1 percent of the population, has it. When a person with celiac disease eats gluten, their immune system overreacts and damages the villi inside the small intestine. Villi—small, finger-like protrusions that help absorb nutrients into the bloodstream—are a critical part of the digestion process, and damaged villi can result in malnourishment.

In the past, it was common for people to suffer from this disorder their whole lives without a diagnosis. Estimates suggest that the average celiac patient still waits between six and ten years before getting a correct diagnosis.

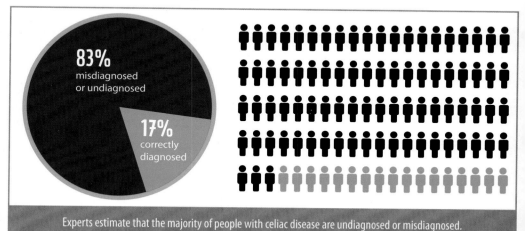

Experts estimate that the majority of people with celiac disease are undiagnosed or misdiagnosed.

The recent focus on the disease and gluten in general has significantly improved the likelihood of being diagnosed early, before serious intestinal damage can occur. However, 83 percent of those with celiac disease remain undiagnosed or misdiagnosed.

In some people, celiac symptoms can happen even if they do not have the disease. Doctors call this non-celiac gluten sensitivity, or NCGS, and it is considered to be as serious a disorder as celiac disease. The symptoms of gluten sensitivity are not triggered by the same kind of autoimmune response as celiac disease, but they have similar effects on the gastrointestinal (GI) tract. The underlying cause of gluten sensitivity is not yet understood, and it even remains a mystery whether the same part of gluten-containing grains causes both celiac and gluten sensitive reactions. In the face of such a seemingly widespread problem, doctors and scientists continue to study the disease and look for a cure, but answers may be far off.

CHAPTER ONE

WHAT CELIAC DISEASE DOES AND HOW TO FIND IT

Despite the recent media explosion about gluten-related disorders, celiac disease remains underdiagnosed. People who suffer from it can go misdiagnosed for more than a decade, trying solution after solution that does not work, from medications to invasive surgeries. The problem lies in the incredible range of symptoms celiac can cause.

Common symptoms include gastrointestinal distress and weight loss, but the vast majority of celiac patients also suffer from seemingly unrelated issues such as depression or dental defects. As a group, few celiac patients are alike, making it difficult for doctors to tell when symptoms are pointing to celiac and when they are pointing to some other disease. The only way to know for sure if someone has celiac is to test for it, and while celiac testing is becoming more often recommended, it is still not most doctors' first instinct when a patient comes in with GI problems.

There are many things, however, that experts do know about celiac disease. They know how celiac operates in the body and how it inflicts damage on the small intestine. They know how to diagnose celiac and what tests are necessary to find answers. Although its symptoms vary, experts are getting closer to a comprehensive list of what doctors should look for when deciding whether a patient should have testing done. The World Gastroenterology Organization categorizes celiac disease into three types: classical, non-classical or atypical, and silent or asymptomatic. This type of knowledge is key to creating a foundation for finding faster diagnostic methods, more effective treatments and, perhaps someday, a cure for gluten-related disorders.

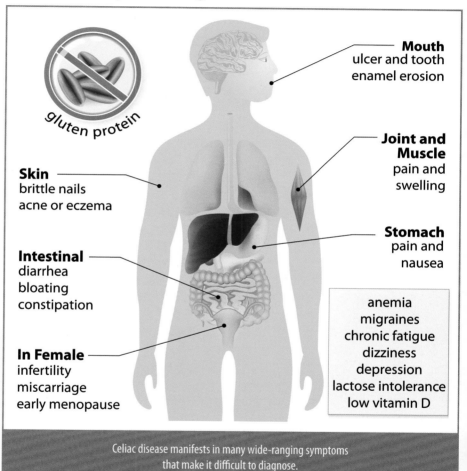

gluten protein

Mouth
ulcer and tooth enamel erosion

Joint and Muscle
pain and swelling

Skin
brittle nails
acne or eczema

Stomach
pain and nausea

Intestinal
diarrhea
bloating
constipation

anemia
migraines
chronic fatigue
dizziness
depression
lactose intolerance
low vitamin D

In Female
infertility
miscarriage
early menopause

Celiac disease manifests in many wide-ranging symptoms that make it difficult to diagnose.

Gluten in the Body

When people eat, food passes through their organs in the following order: mouth, esophagus, stomach, small intestine, large intestine, and anus. The pancreas, liver, and gallbladder are important organs in the digestive system as well, but food does not pass through them. The general purpose of the digestive system is to break down food so the body can absorb the nutrients out of it, which is vital to staying healthy and keeping the systems of the body moving.

The digestive system is not perfect, though. Gluten—or more precisely, gliadin, one of the proteins that makes up gluten—is incredibly difficult for the body to break down. On its way through the GI tract, gliadin meets up with an enzyme called transglutaminase 2 (TG2), which makes it even harder to digest. Eventually, the body deals with the problem and simply gets rid of gliadin as waste, but in people with celiac disease, something goes wrong as this protein-enzyme mixture lingers in the digestive tract.

Immune cells in the small intestine are generally very good at telling the difference between a threat and a non-threat, but celiac disease makes the membrane receptors in some of these cells easier to trick into believing that gliadin is a potentially dangerous substance. This by itself would be enough to trigger an immune response as the cells attack the substance they see as a threat, but the unfortunate thing about gliadin is that it prefers to latch onto these particularly sensitive cells after it has been chemically altered by TG2. An inflammatory autoimmune response is almost guaranteed after that because the gliadin seems even more unknown to the body.

When the immune system reacts to gliadin, it produces two kinds of antibodies known as immunoglobulin A (IgA) and immunoglobulin G (IgG). IgA is the main troublemaker for celiac patients. It has direct contact with the lining and mucus membrane of the small intestine, and when celiac is activated by the arrival of gluten, IgA attacks the villi in the small intestine instead of the perceived threat of gliadin.

Unfortunately, this only makes it harder for the body to properly digest gliadin.

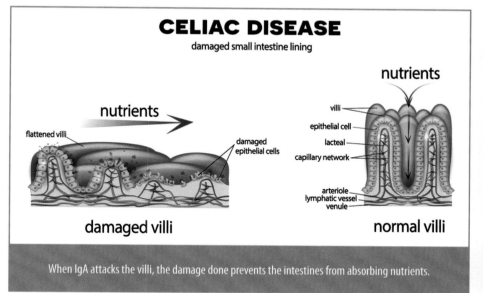

When IgA attacks the villi, the damage done prevents the intestines from absorbing nutrients.

Getting a Diagnosis

Being tested for celiac disease is not necessary for everyone, but there are a few guidelines that doctors tend to follow when deciding who should be referred for screening. The first and most obvious is that anyone over the age of three who is showing signs of celiac should be tested. If a doctor suspects celiac, they will want to have their suspicions confirmed or denied by a laboratory. The second group of people who should be screened are the first-degree relatives of anyone who is diagnosed with celiac. Depending on the study, close relatives have between a 1 in 10 and a 1 in 20 chance of also having the disease, whereas the general population has only a 1 in 100 chance. Anyone who has "type 1 diabetes mellitus, autoimmune thyroid disease, autoimmune liver disease, Down syndrome, Turner syndrome, Williams syndrome, and selective immunoglobulin A (IgA) deficiency,"[3] as well as any other associated autoimmune disease should also be tested for celiac. These diseases can be complicated by celiac, so it is important to rule it out as a factor to consider during treatment.

There are two ways to screen for celiac disease: blood testing and genetic testing. There are currently three blood tests that will measure the amount of IgA in someone's system. Total IgA, IgA-tTG, and IgA-EMA tests can all be performed if the doctor wishes, and if IgA in the blood is deficient for some reason, IgG/IgA-DGP and IgG-AGA tests may be done to measure levels of IgG. These two antibodies in the blood are the only indicators that celiac is most likely the issue. Genetic testing can tell the doctor if celiac is even a possibility, since certain genes must be present for celiac to occur, but it cannot tell them if celiac has manifested in someone who is predisposed to it. In other words, although someone may carry the genes responsible for celiac disease, they may not ever suffer from the symptoms of the disease.

However, if either of these tests come back positive for signs of celiac, the doctor will most likely order an endoscopic biopsy of the small intestine to confirm the diagnosis. This is a low-risk, 15-minute procedure. During an endoscopy, the patient is sedated, or put to sleep, and a tiny camera on the end of a very thin tube is inserted through the mouth and snaked all the way through the digestive system to the small intestine. The doctor will then examine the walls of the intestine for villi damage and will likely do a biopsy, which involves taking a small tissue sample to examine it more closely. If damage to the villi is apparent when the tissue sample is studied under a microscope, then the doctor will diagnose celiac disease.

The Problem of Self-Diagnosis

Because of how little information doctors have about celiac disease, getting a diagnosis can be difficult, so some people have begun to diagnose themselves. With the internet's help, they find and latch onto the words "celiac disease" or "non-celiac gluten sensitivity" to describe the cause of their symptoms, even when they have not been tested for either of these conditions. They then begin a gluten-free diet without talking to their doctor about it first; sometimes their doctor may even suggest a gluten-free diet without doing the proper tests to determine whether it is actually necessary. According to one Australian study of people who had self-diagnosed NCGS, one out of four subjects showed no change in their symptoms after switching to a gluten-free diet, meaning that gluten was not the real problem. "This is a common scenario for people with fructose malabsorption," said Dr. Amy Burkhart, who specializes in digestive health. "Instituting a gluten-free diet will help but not eliminate symptoms when the real trigger is the carbohydrate component, not the gluten protein."[1] Other factors may also be causing the problem, and self-diagnosing prevents someone from treating the real issue.

1. Amy Burkhart, "Self-Diagnosis of Gluten Sensitivity: Four Alarming Trends," The Celiac MD, accessed on November 15, 2017. theceliacmd.com/2014/05/self-diagnosis-gluten-sensitivity-four-alarming-trends/.

Celiac Symptoms

Since celiac disease attacks the small intestine, the most common and easily recognizable symptoms have to do with the digestive system. In cases of classical celiac disease, patients generally have diarrhea (too much water in the feces), steatorrhea (too much fat in the feces), and weight loss, all of which are indicators that a person is not absorbing nutrients properly—a situation known as malabsorption. Abdominal bloating or gas sometimes accompanies classical celiac as well. In general, watery or fatty stools are signs that the intestines are not absorbing fluids or fat the way they should, and in celiac patients, this is due to the damaged villi in the small intestine. These issues also cause abdominal cramping, making celiac not only inconvenient but painful, too.

Although some people actively seek out weight loss for personal or health reasons, weight loss in celiac patients is a sign of malnutrition, and malnutrition has serious effects on the whole body.

Malabsorption of nutrients in celiac disease sufferers can lead to vitamin deficiencies, malnutrition, and weight loss.

Because the intestines are not able to draw the nutrients out of food, the body can quickly become deficient in vitamins, minerals, and other substances necessary to properly function. This makes celiac patients more susceptible to other diseases, such as cancer, diabetes, tuberculosis, pneumonia, and disorders in the kidneys and bowels. Weight loss can also have mental and social effects, as celiac patient Jaclyn remembered from her childhood:

> Before I was diagnosed with celiac disease in 2005, anyone I met thought I had an eating disorder. I was told I was paranoid, but I could feel people's eyes on me. I never wanted to wear

anything that showed my legs or my arms. I would go out in 90-degree weather in baggy sweatpants and an oversized sweatshirt, not caring if I produced buckets and buckets of sweat. I was so self-conscious about my weight and how others perceived my situation. Being able to hear whispers at school and in public about my stick thin legs and my toothpick arms made the situation worse.[4]

Struggling with the physical symptoms of celiac disease is difficult enough, but trying to maintain a healthy mental state at the same time is sometimes even more of a battle.

In non-classical or atypical celiac cases, patients have milder GI-related symptoms and do not show the classic signs of malabsorption. Instead, celiac manifests in many other ways—so many other ways, in fact, that the symptoms sometimes seem unrelated. The Celiac Disease Foundation lists, among other symptoms,

abdominal distension [swelling] and pain … iron-deficiency anemia, chronic fatigue, chronic migraine, peripheral neuropathy (tingling, numbness, or pain in hands or feet), unexplained chronic hypertransaminasemia (elevated liver enzymes), reduced bone mass and bone fractures, and vitamin deficiency (folic acid and B12), late menarche/early menopause and unexplained infertility, dental enamel defects, depression and anxiety, dermatitis herpetiformis (itchy skin rash).[5]

The number and range of symptoms of atypical celiac disease make it much harder to diagnose. Every case has a different combination of signs, and in many situations, the combination of symptoms a celiac sufferer exhibits looks like a completely different disease, leading to misdiagnosis.

Dermatitis Herpetiformis

Also known as DH or Duhring's disease, dermatitis herpetiformis is a skin rash that resembles herpes lesions, although it has nothing to do with the herpes virus.

It affects 10 to 15 percent of people with celiac disease, typically first appears between the ages of 30 and 40, and frequently accompanies celiac when there are no digestive symptoms. When a gluten sensitive person eats gluten, their intestines produce antibodies—specifically IgA—to protect themselves. However, this particular type of antibody often reacts with the skin, causing a rash to form on the elbows, knees, buttocks, and back. Doctors generally prescribe dapsone, an antibacterial drug, to clear up the rash. Combined with a gluten-free diet, dapsone works on dermatitis herpetiformis in 48 to 72 hours.

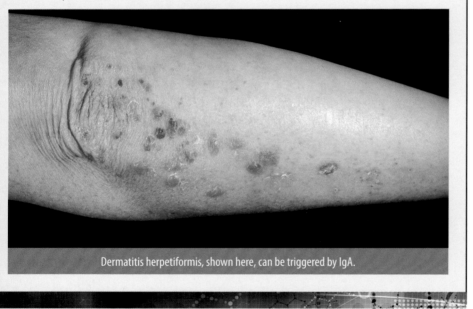

Dermatitis herpetiformis, shown here, can be triggered by IgA.

Being Asymptomatic

Like atypical celiac, silent or asymptomatic celiac disease is difficult for doctors to diagnose, but for a different reason. Instead of having many seemingly unrelated symptoms, people with silent celiac have no symptoms at all, although they will test positive for it if they are sent in for screening. Diagnosing silent celiac often happens almost by accident, when a person is diagnosed with a related illness such as thyroid disease or anemia and the doctor refers them for celiac screening as a precaution. Other people are diagnosed because they chose to get the recommended precautionary tests after someone in their immediate family was diagnosed with celiac. Besides these scenarios, there is no way for doctors to know if someone has silent celiac, and therefore they do not know to have them tested.

However, just because silent celiac has no outward symptoms does not mean it has no effects. Even with no symptoms present, damage to the small intestine still takes place and makes the digestive system less effective. This is a health risk, symptoms or no symptoms, and it is recommended that people with silent celiac stick to a gluten-free diet like anyone else with the disease. Not only does it prevent further intestinal damage, but a 2011 Finnish study suggests that it may also improve the quality of asymptomatic celiac patients' lives:

> *The researchers split the group in two, assigning half of the patients to a gluten-free diet and the other half to a regular, gluten-containing diet. They then tracked them for a year through surveys designed to evaluate both gastrointestinal symptoms and health-related quality of life.*
>
> *The study found that survey scores—both in symptoms and quality of life—improved in the group following the gluten-free diet, while scores stayed the same in the group on the regular diet ... Even though the group following the gluten-free diet hadn't noticed symptoms before, they reported seeing some minor symptoms—including reflux, bloating, abdominal distention and flatulence— clear up when eating gluten-free.[6]*

The study showed that even seemingly asymptomatic patients had some reaction to gluten, although it was not severe enough to prompt them to seek medical help. Their mild symptoms were just a part of their lives until they went gluten-free. For this reason, as well as the obvious bonus of not destroying the small intestine, doctors recommend a gluten-free diet for everyone with celiac, even if it is not for the treatment of observable symptoms.

Children's Celiac

People used to believe that celiac disease was exclusively a childhood illness. It is now known that celiac affects adults and children alike, but for a long time, children simply suffered with it because their parents thought they would eventually grow out of it. Today, parents often know more about celiac, and most will actively try to seek out answers if their child is clearly sick. However, identifying celiac in children can be difficult because it does not always present in the same ways as it does in adults.

Children with celiac have only a 20 to 30 percent chance of having stomach symptoms, although they are more likely to have diarrhea than adults. The most common, or at least the most noticeable, symptoms in children are decreased appetite, failure to thrive—a term doctors use to refer to children who do not gain weight on the same schedule as others their same age—and a swollen belly. Like adults, they can also have anemia, bloating, fatigue, and dermatitis herpetiformis.

Celiac affects children differently depending on how old they are. Infants and toddlers are at a considerable risk because of how hard celiac makes gaining weight, and gaining weight and muscle mass are of the utmost importance during these early years of life. Vomiting, irritability, and poor growth because of malnutrition are some of the warning signs of celiac in children up to three years old. Unfortunately, even if a baby is showing signs of gluten intolerance from the time they are introduced to foods other than milk, normal methods of testing may not be able to diagnose them.

It often takes several months of eating cereal before a baby begins to develop the antibodies associated with celiac disease, making it very difficult to diagnose in children under three.

According to the University of Chicago Celiac Disease Center, "Children must be eating wheat or barley-based cereals for some time, up to several months, before they can generate an autoimmune response to gluten that shows up in testing."[7] In cases concerning such young children, doctors will generally recommend genetic testing for celiac to narrow down the possible causes of their symptoms.

Like adults, older children and teenagers who show atypical symptoms of celiac are more commonly undiagnosed or misdiagnosed. While digestive symptoms such as diarrhea sometimes lessen as a child grows older, delayed growth once again becomes a main concern. Adolescents with celiac disease may experience delayed puberty because they are not getting the nutrients their bodies need to start the process. Anxiety and depression are also common among teenagers with celiac. The physical and emotional stress of having celiac disease, as well as the chemical imbalance it causes, may set off adolescents who are predisposed to these mood disorders. No matter the cause, however, it is important that teenagers who find themselves experiencing panic attacks, anxiety, or depression talk to someone

Gluten and ADHD

ADHD, or attention-deficit/hyperactivity disorder, affects between 5 and 11 percent of school-aged children, and in some cases, symptoms persist into adulthood. Impulsivity, being easily distracted, and difficulty concentrating are the most common and well-known signs of ADHD, but for a long time, people have claimed that switching to a gluten-free diet can lessen these symptoms. Although the results in people with ADHD and non-celiac gluten sensitivity are less conclusive, one study found a link between ADHD and celiac disease:

> In one study, researchers tested 67 people with ADHD for celiac disease. Study participants ranged in age from 7 to 42. A total of 15% tested positive for celiac disease. That's far higher than the incidence of celiac in the general population, which is about 1%.

> Once they started on a gluten-free diet, the patients or their parents reported significant improvements in their behavior and functioning, and these improvements were backed up by ratings on a check list physicians use to monitor the severity of ADHD symptoms.[1]

Although some people's ADHD symptoms may be improved through a gluten-free diet, it is important to note that not all instances of ADHD are related to gluten. A gluten-free diet is not a proven "cure" for ADHD, and researchers are still searching for the cause of this disorder. Celiac disease and ADHD may be related, but further study is necessary to verify the outcome of this particular study and to determine whether one causes the other.

1. Jane Anderson, "Do Celiac and Gluten Sensitivity Raise the Odds of ADHD?," Verywell, September 11, 2017. www.verywell.com/gluten-and-adhd-562627.

about it. A doctor may be able to help, and if the root of the problem is celiac, the fix could be as simple as a gluten-free diet.

Gluten Sensitivity Symptoms

Gluten sensitivity looks almost identical to celiac on the surface. Symptoms such as "'foggy mind', depression, ADHD-like behavior, abdominal pain, bloating, diarrhea, constipation, headaches, bone or joint pain, and chronic fatigue"[8] are all characteristics of both celiac and non-celiac gluten sensitivity. However, extra-intestinal, or non-GI tract, symptoms tend to be more common in NCGS patients. This may be because gluten sensitivity is not triggered by an autoimmune response the way celiac is, but is instead caused by something known as an innate-immune response. This does not produce the same antibodies as a full-blown autoimmune response and is therefore often considered less serious.

For a long time, doctors believed that although NCGS presented in the same ways as celiac, it was a less severe condition. In 2012, a paper entitled "The Oslo Definitions for Coeliac Disease and Related Terms" was published in an attempt to regulate the language doctors use to talk about celiac disease and other gluten-related disorders. Although it was well-received and the terms it presented were generally adopted by the medical community, its definition of gluten sensitivity enforced the inaccurate belief that there was no effect on the intestines associated with NCGS. In 2016, however, a paper published by the Columbia University Medical Center disproved this assumption. Even if doctors cannot see it right away, NCGS triggers "a systemic immune reaction and accompanying intestinal cell damage,"[9] although it is much more subtle than celiac disease.

Having NCGS puts patients into a strange no-man's-land. While there is clearly something wrong with them, there is almost no way to diagnose NCGS for sure. The antibodies associated with celiac disease are not found in their blood, and the histamines associated with a wheat allergy are absent as well, but eating a gluten-free diet generally relieves these people of their symptoms. This is baffling to health care professionals, many of whom are divided on the subject of NCGS. Some believe that gluten sensitivity is an overinflated diagnosis; for instance, Mary Schluckebier, executive director of the Celiac Support Association, believes the rising number of people with gluten sensitivity are being given that label by doctors simply because they demand an answer to their problems. "A patient goes

People with NCGS often find themselves struggling to get a diagnosis from a medical community with very divided opinions on exactly what NCGS is and whether it exists at all.

to the doctor, and they want a diagnosis," she said in an interview. "'Don't tell me I don't have this—give me a name for it.' So doctors came up for a name for it. I think it was a way to appease impatient patients. I don't know how to say that nicely."[10] Most likely, NCGS is related to a different family of diseases, but doctors have yet to discover its secrets. In the end, doctors have to believe what their patients tell them, and if someone is experiencing symptoms with no apparent cause, it is up to the medical community to dig deeper and find the problem.

CHAPTER TWO

LOOKING FOR A CAUSE

Although finding treatments and managing the symptoms of celiac disease are of the utmost importance, scientists are also interested in discovering what makes celiac happen. The simplest answer is genetics, but that is not the whole story. A person without the genes that cause celiac will never get the disorder, but even most people who do have the genes will never get it. This makes the actual cause of celiac something sufferers encounter at some point in their lives. A trigger of some kind is needed to set off the disease. Researchers have discovered links between the onset of celiac and GI infections, gut bacteria, and stress, but there are few definitive answers. Finding those answers could unlock more effective treatment methods and possibly even a preventive measure or a cure, which is why researchers continue their work.

Genetics

The one culprit researchers know for sure causes celiac disease is genetics. Genes are the instructions for building living organisms; they are made up of deoxyribonucleic acid (DNA), which is the basic material that makes up every cell in every plant and animal on Earth. People inherit their genes from their biological parents, both of whom donate half of their genetic code to create a new code in their child. Unfortunately, this means that many diseases can travel through families, from one generation to the next, through sequences of DNA that make family members predisposed to certain disorders. Celiac disease is the result of the presence of two genes, HLA-DQ2 and HLA-DQ8. HLA stands for "human leukocyte antigens," and a subset of this family of genes is typically involved with genetic autoimmune diseases. According to Dr. Sheila Crowe, a professor at the University of Virginia, "95 percent of people with celiac disease have genes that include H.L.A. DQ2, and 5 percent have genes with H.L.A. DQ8."[11] Without these genes, there is no way someone can develop celiac disease, which is why genetic testing can be important when trying to diagnose it.

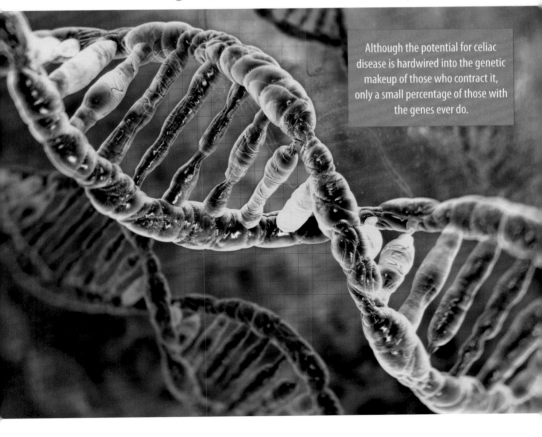

Although the potential for celiac disease is hardwired into the genetic makeup of those who contract it, only a small percentage of those with the genes ever do.

Having these genes, however, is not a guarantee that celiac disease will show up. "Thirty to 40 percent of people in the United States have one

Genetic Testing

As genetics become an increasingly important part of diagnosing diseases, it is becoming more necessary that both doctors and patients know how genetic testing is done. Informed consent—giving permission for a doctor to do a test after being told how and why the test is being performed—is a vital part of managing one's own health. Unfortunately, some doctors are not very knowledgeable about or comfortable with genetic testing, so it is difficult for patients to get enough information about it to make an informed decision. For instance, in 1951, a woman named Henrietta Lacks died of cervical cancer, and cells from her tumor became the first to be kept alive in a laboratory. Researchers all over the world wanted to study the cells, so doctors began calling Henrietta's family members to give blood samples. However, they did not clearly explain what they were doing, so in 1974, Henrietta's daughter Deborah gave blood thinking she was being tested for the same cancer her mother had. She asked the doctor for an explanation about the blood tests, and he gave her a textbook about genetic testing filled with difficult medical words that Deborah did not understand. When she and her other family members found out their blood was actually being used for medical research—and that they were not given any of the money that research generated—they were very upset. They had given their consent for the tests to be performed, but it was not informed consent because they did not understand what they were saying yes to.

To combat this type of misinformation, the medical community is trying to educate the public on genetic research so patients can go into their appointments armed with knowledge. The Genetics Home Reference of the U.S. National Library of Medicine explained the basics of a genetic test so it is easy to understand:

> Genetic tests are performed on a sample of blood, hair, skin, amniotic fluid (the fluid that surrounds a fetus during pregnancy), or other tissue. For example, a procedure called a buccal smear uses a small brush or cotton swab to collect a sample of cells from the inside surface of the cheek. The sample is sent to a laboratory where technicians look for specific changes in chromosomes, DNA, or proteins, depending on the suspected disorder. The laboratory reports the test results in writing to a person's doctor or genetic counselor, or directly to the patient if requested.[1]

1. "How Is Genetic Testing Done?," Genetics Home Reference, January 23, 2018. ghr.nlm.nih.gov/primer/testing/procedure.

or both of the genes called HLA-DQ2 or DQ8, which are the ones associated with celiac disease," said Amy Leger, who began to research the genetics behind celiac because of a long family history of the disease. "The National Institutes of Health says only about 3 percent of those with the genes actually get celiac disease."[12] Ultimately, genetic testing is only good for assessing whether it is possible for someone to have celiac disease, so it is a tool that is used far less frequently than people might think.

Genetic testing is not used as often as it could be to diagnose celiac disease, due in part to the cost associated with the test and to many doctors' inexperience in interpreting and utilizing the results.

According to Leger, 20 percent or fewer patients of a gastroenterologist will be genetically tested for celiac, even though it can be a very useful tool in making a diagnosis. There are two reasons for this. The first is that there is a good chance a person's health insurance will not cover the test. Genetic testing is sometimes not covered at all, and other times, the insurance claim will be denied because there is no drug or surgical treatment for celiac even if they find the genetic markers for it. To an insurance company, this means money wasted since the disease being tested for cannot be treated with medicine. The second reason is that many doctors do not know what to do with genetic test results. However, there are commercially available genetic testing kits that patients can use themselves, removing the doctor as the middleman between them and the answers they are looking for. Even if these tests cannot give people a diagnosis, they may be able to give them some peace of mind or the motivation to ask their doctor for blood tests looking for celiac.

Gastrointestinal Infections

Besides genetics, researchers believe one of the major factors in the development of celiac disease could be a history of viral infections in the GI tract. Since both trigger a response from the immune system in the same general area, celiac and GI infections are clearly related on some level, but doctors have only recently begun to figure out how. In 2014, researchers at the University of Chicago Celiac Disease Center started looking for signs of previous infections in intestinal biopsies of celiac patients. What they often found were immune system molecules known as type-1 interferon or type-1 IFN, which are associated with viral infections, proving that a large number of celiac sufferers also had stomach or intestinal infections at some point. "This continuous stimulation could lead to a loss of tolerance towards gluten and the development of the disease in a subset of individuals,"[13] explained Dr. Valentina Discepolo, a postdoctoral fellow at the University of Chicago Celiac Disease Center. She went into detail about the biological process behind this loss of tolerance:

One crucial concept is that in healthy individuals, the intestinal mucosal immune system continuously samples what comes in contact with our intestine (foreign as well as indigenous microbes and food antigens) and decides what to tolerate and what to fight. In other words, there is a dynamic and continuous balance between regulatory (promoting tolerance) and inflammatory (promoting inflammation) responses towards antigens in the gut ... It seems that in genetically susceptible individuals, some environmental factors may disrupt the balance between tolerance and inflammation and enhance an inflammatory response that, once started, could be self-perpetuating and would need the removal of the causative agent (in celiac disease, gluten) to be switched off.[14]

Put simply, the immune system may become oversensitive if it is exposed to a virus multiple times. In people who are genetically predisposed to celiac, this means that too many GI infections could activate the disease and change the immune response to attack gluten as if it were a virus.

However, proving that one illness causes another is sometimes much more difficult than it would seem. One study is not enough to base medical practice on. In the years since researchers first began to draw connections between celiac disease and viral infections, investigations have continued to support the theory, but no official relationship has been declared. One such study was done in Germany in 2017, examining the medical history of infants in Bavaria born between 2005 and 2007. Researchers found that children who had a GI infection during their first year of life had a higher rate of developing celiac than the average child and that the likelihood of developing celiac increased if the infection recurred. Not only does

Reovirus

While studying reoviruses—a type of virus that generally either shows no symptoms or presents like the common cold—Dr. Terence Dermody, head of the Department of Pediatrics at the University of Pittsburgh, and a team of researchers from other universities discovered that they may trigger celiac disease. In genetically engineered mice, being infected with a reovirus and then fed gluten caused their immune systems to react in a similar way to a human with celiac.

A second stage of the study revealed that human celiac patients have two to five times more antibodies specific to reoviruses than the average person. Although proving a causal relationship between the two illnesses will take years of clinical trials, researchers hope that drawing such a connection could prompt parents to have their children genetically tested for celiac and vaccinated against reoviruses if they carry the genes for it. In the long run, this might prevent many people from developing celiac disease even if they are predisposed to it.

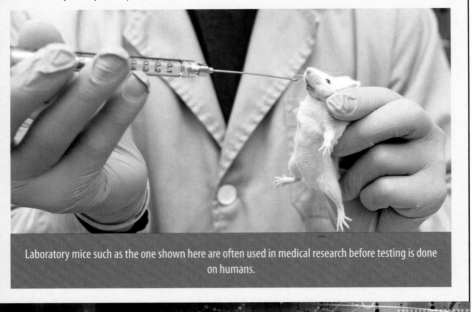

Laboratory mice such as the one shown here are often used in medical research before testing is done on humans.

this study support the previous theory, but because there was no consistent pattern as to what kind of GI infection the children had, it also suggests that a "persistent state of inflammation"[15] is to blame rather than a specific virus or bacteria. A similar study looking at celiac in American military personnel also seems to suggest that infections can trigger the disease. Out of 455 subjects with celiac disease, 172 had infectious gastroenteritis, or the stomach flu, sometime within two years before their diagnosis. The overall impression from these studies is that GI infections have a larger part to play in the development of celiac than most people currently realize.

Gut Bacteria

Although people typically hear about bacteria in the context of infections and illnesses, bacteria can also be good. People's bodies are full of bacteria that help the organs function normally, and the digestive system is no exception. In the stomach, a community of different bacteria known generally as gut flora help with digestion, absorb nutrients, and produce vitamins B and K. They also neutralize things that are bad for humans, such as toxins and harmful bacteria that people sometimes ingest without meaning to. This entire system of gut bacteria is called a microbiome, and studies have shown that the balance of the microbiome in the GI tract is key to digestive health. Unfortunately, other studies have revealed that people with celiac disease almost always have an imbalance of gut flora, as well as less diversity among them. This is a symptom of the disease, but it may also contribute to triggering it. Because the processes of the stomach microbiome are so important to the function of the intestines, researchers believe that a gut imbalance might leave predisposed people less protected against the irritants that set off the immune system in the small intestine.

A study published in 2014 proposes that the bacterium *Helicobacter pylori* may have a relationship with the onset of celiac disease. Dr. Benjamin

Lebwohl, assistant professor of Clinical Medicine and Epidemiology at Columbia University, and a number of other researchers began looking for answers when it came to their attention that the incidence of celiac disease in the United States increased when *H. pylori* became harder to find in the average person's stomach microbiome. By examining stomach and intestinal biopsies, "Lebwohl and his colleagues found a strong, inverse association between *H. pylori* presence and CD [celiac disease]. In patients without CD, *H. pylori* prevalence was found to be 8.8% while it was only 4.4% in patients with CD."[16] Although this difference does not seem like much, this means people with celiac disease have half the amount of *H. pylori* as someone without it. However, other studies on the same topic are inconclusive, making it difficult to say whether *H. pylori* is as significant as Lebwohl and his team made it out to be. Research into this particular bacterium is still going on years later, so it is not out of the question for a major discovery about it to emerge eventually.

Another, more recent study focused on *Pseudomonas aeruginosa*. This bacterium is found in abundance in the gut microbiomes of celiac patients, but it is less common in people without the disease. Instead, it seems, people without celiac have more *Lactobacillus*, a different kind of bacterium that is often used as a probiotic—a substance that helps increase the amount of good bacteria in the gut. To observe the effects of these two bacteria, researchers harvested them from humans and put them in mice. After feeding the mice gluten, the researchers came to a huge discovery:

> When the bacteria under study encountered gluten, they produced molecules called peptides. Knowing that different peptides talk differently

to immune cells—those provoking a stronger immune response are called more "immuno-genic"—the researchers tested how the peptides reacted with blood immune cells isolated from people with CD.

They found the peptides produced by the celiac-sourced Pseudomonas aeruginosa *did something interesting: they activated gluten-specific immune cells, meaning the peptides were highly immunogenic. The* Lactobacillus *species from the healthy people, on the other hand, were able to degrade these peptides in order to decrease the immune reaction.*[17]

From this study, researchers have concluded that *P. aeruginosa* is a key part of understanding celiac disease, even if it does not directly cause it. Figuring out more about how celiac works, as well as figuring out different ways of neutralizing its effects, is equally as important as finding its cause.

Stress

It has been a long-held belief in the celiac community that stress can induce the disease, but it was not until 2013 that scientific data backed up that claim. In one study that year, researchers in Italy compared recently diagnosed celiac patients to a control group of people diagnosed with gastroesophageal reflux disease, or GERD, a GI disorder that is not related to the autoimmune system the way celiac is. Using a questionnaire that asked about "changes in employment, education, relationships, financial status, health status, and living spaces, deaths in close relatives, criminal accusations and convictions, family and social problems and marital problems"[18] that had occurred up to a year before their diagnosis, the researchers were able to draw conclusions about the connection between intense stress and celiac disease:

> *The researchers found that those with celiac disease were statistically more likely to have experienced one of these "life events" in the year prior to diagnosis when compared to those in the GERD control group.*
>
> *This effect was even stronger when the researchers limited their analysis to those who began experiencing celiac disease symptoms only in the year prior to diagnosis—in other words, when their symptoms appeared in the same time frame as the stressful life event.*[19]

Increased stress at home and work appears to be a factor in triggering the onset of celiac disease.

One speculation researchers have made based on the study's results is that stress disturbs the gut microbiome and throws it off balance, leaving the small intestine vulnerable. Although this study presents convincing results, it has been the only one of its kind, meaning further studies are necessary to confirm its findings.

An interesting result of this study was that women seemed to be more susceptible to stress-induced celiac disease than men, especially when they reported a pregnancy in the year before their celiac diagnosis. Another Italian study found that "85.7% of women received their celiac diagnosis following their first pregnancy."[20] On one hand, it is entirely possible that these women had

Emotional Changes

To function properly, the brain needs nourishment, but malabsorption caused by celiac disease can weaken the supply of vitamins and minerals gained from food. Imbalanced brain chemistry due to malnourishment can cause psychological problems, and several mental health issues are often reported as symptoms of celiac. These include:

- *Mood changes*

- *Anxiety*

- *Fatigue*

- *Difficulties with concentration and attention*

- *Sleep difficulties*

- *Decrease [in] appetite*[1]

Children can also experience behavioral problems for this same reason. Poor brain function, combined with the stress of a celiac diagnosis and the beginning of a gluten-free diet, can sometimes lead to depression and anxiety that continue even after gluten consumption has stopped. However, persistent psychological symptoms may indicate the need for mental health evaluation in addition to a gluten-free diet.

1. "Celiac Disease and Mental Health," Celiac Disease Foundation, accessed on January 12, 2018. celiac.org/celiac-disease/understanding-celiac-disease-2/child-mental-health/.

celiac before they were pregnant, but increased health monitoring finally brought it to their doctor's attention. It is also possible, however, that the stress of pregnancy triggered gluten sensitivity. Pregnancy and birth are extremely stressful both mentally and physically, and they often change a woman's body chemistry permanently. Therefore, it is not out of the question that these intense emotional and hormonal fluctuations could trigger celiac.

FODMAPs

Since it seems to be separate from celiac disease, the cause of gluten sensitivity has puzzled doctors for years. Although gluten appears, on the surface, to be the issue, gluten-free diets do not always clear up symptoms of gluten sensitivity. However, as more people experiment with their diets to treat their symptoms, researchers are realizing that gluten may not be to blame. Instead, the problem may lie with FODMAPs. According to the Gluten Intolerance Group,

> *FODMAP stands for Fermentable-Oligosaccharide-Disaccharide-Monosaccharide-And-Polyols. Essentially, FODMAPs are certain types of sugars and shorter chain carbohydrates. They are found in a broad range of foods, including some items from each of the following categories: fruits, vegetables, nuts, seeds, grains and grain-based products, dairy and dairy alternatives, sugars and sweeteners.*[21]

These molecules are particularly difficult for the small intestine to absorb and often ferment in the large intestine, leading to most of the GI symptoms commonly associated with celiac disease.

Scientists propose that the reason people with "gluten sensitivity" feel better on a gluten-free

For people with non-celiac gluten sensitivity, it is possible that gluten is not the culprit, but rather foods from across the spectrum that ferment in their gut.

diet is because wheat, barley, and rye all contain fermentable oligosaccharide, the FO in FODMAP, as well as gluten. Cutting out gluten also cuts out a sizeable amount of the FODMAPs in one's diet, leading people who do not know about FODMAPs to believe the problem was gluten and label themselves "gluten sensitive." However, since the list of FODMAPs ranges over so many different types of food, eliminating gluten may only lessen symptoms and does not address the real source of the issue. This is not to say that NCGS does not exist, but it is likely that it is much rarer than statistics currently indicate. Without real proof from a lab test, it is almost impossible to say for sure what is causing someone's GI symptoms, and there has not yet been a test invented for detecting NCGS. Fortunately, dietary changes and new treatments can help manage the symptoms of both NCGS and celiac disease, preventing damage to the GI tract and allowing patients to live the way they want to.

CHAPTER THREE

MANAGING CELIAC DISEASE

Because there is no cure for celiac disease, managing it and preventing it from doing further damage to the small intestine is the only way to proceed after a celiac diagnosis. Currently, the only treatment for celiac is a strict, lifelong gluten-free diet. There are no medications or surgeries that will treat it or repair the damage to the small intestine. After following a gluten-free diet, celiac patients should see and feel their symptoms clearing up, and eventually, the small intestine may even heal from the immune system's attacks.

However, just because a gluten-free diet is the only treatment for celiac does not mean it is the only thing that needs to be done to recover from years of malabsorption and GI tract imbalance. Dietary supplements and home remedies can significantly improve celiac patients' overall health and quality of life. Mental health is also an important aspect to be taken care of while adjusting to gluten-free living. All in all, the main goal of managing celiac disease is creating a gluten-free environment where the body can heal, but also making sure that life going forward is as free of symptoms and unnecessary stress as possible.

Following Up

Horror stories about being abandoned by doctors after a celiac diagnosis are abundant on the internet. One anonymous woman struggled with celiac symptoms for years and had to force her doctor to send for blood tests to see if she had the disease. After the test came back positive, the woman recalled, "I asked her what happens now. She said you go and live a gluten free life. I said what about follow up? A referral to a dietician? Another scope? She told me to Google it. She said all of the information that I needed was on the internet."[22] Doctors who feel this way do unfortunately exist, but being well-informed about what follow-up should be like can help celiac patients find the help they need.

Figuring out how one's doctor feels about treating celiac disease is relatively easy during the diagnosis appointment. During that first appointment, besides recommending a strict gluten-free diet, a

It is important for a patient with celiac disease to feel that their doctor is actively assisting in their treatment.

doctor should order a multitude of tests: a bone densitometry test to make sure malabsorption has not interfered with bone strength, anti-DGP IgA and anti-tTg IgA tests to find base levels of immunoglobulin A, and routine blood tests such as "blood cell count, iron studies, vitamin B studies, thyroid functions tests with thyrotropin, liver enzymes, calcium, phosphate, 25-hydroxy vitamin D, copper, and zinc levels"[23] to assess shortages of vitamins and minerals. These tests may sound confusing and scary, but in practice, the patient only has to have an X-ray taken and have some blood drawn. A good doctor will be willing and able to explain each test in further detail. They may also refer newly diagnosed celiac patients to a dietitian and a mental health professional, prescribe a gluten-free multivitamin, and recommend family screening to catch other cases of celiac. In general, it should feel like the doctor is actively working to make sure their patient is taken care of. If it does not seem like the doctor cares, then celiac patients are within their rights to find a different doctor who will actually help them.

Three to six months after a celiac diagnosis, and then again six months later, new celiac patients should go in for follow-up exams. The doctor will do a complete physical, discuss any symptoms the patient may still be having, send for anti-DGP IgA and anti-tTg IgA tests again to make sure immunoglobulin A levels have gone down, and have blood tests taken again to make sure vitamin and mineral levels are better. After a year of a gluten-free diet, the results of celiac patients' IgA test should be completely negative, meaning that these antibodies are no longer being produced. Every year after the first year, all these assessments should be made again, including bone densitometry if the original test came back abnormal and an intestinal biopsy every three to five years to make sure the small intestine is healthy.

Health Care Practitioner Directory

Because finding a doctor who can help celiac sufferers successfully manage their disease is sometimes difficult, the Celiac Disease Foundation has compiled a searchable database of physicians who are willing and qualified to treat celiac disease and gluten sensitivity of all kinds. "The Directory provides basic practice information and verification of valid license/registration," according to the webpage. "The Directory also lists if a practitioner is a CDF Medical Advisory Board member, practices at a Celiac Disease Center or has Continuing Education in Celiac Disease."[1] This way, gluten-sensitive patients all across America can find a doctor who is well-suited to them and their individual situation.

1. "Find a Healthcare Practitioner," Celiac Disease Foundation, accessed on December 26, 2017. celiac.org/celiac-disease/resources/provider-directory/.

Talking to a Dietitian

Both the National Institutes of Health (NIH) and the Academy of Nutrition and Dietetics recommend seeing a dietitian after being diagnosed with celiac disease. Some doctors believe referring their patients to a dietitian is not worthwhile since the internet has so much information about going gluten-free, but many people find themselves lost when it comes to completely changing their diet. The internet is full of conflicting opinions, so figuring out whom to trust can be confusing, and bad information can lead to getting "glutened," or unknowingly eating something with gluten in it and triggering symptoms.

When dealing with celiac disease, a dietitian's main job is to work with their patient on coming up with a nutritional plan that will keep them away from gluten but make sure they are getting the nutrients they need. "A registered dietitian would advise you on gluten-free meal plans, the consumption of whole and enriched gluten-free grains, the addition of multivitamins and mineral supplements (calcium, Vitamin D, iron) and how to read labels to determine if a food is gluten free,"[24] wrote Pam Cureton, a clinical and research dietitian, on the *Gluten-Free Living* website. Every

Getting Glutened

After being on a gluten-free diet for a while, people with celiac disease generally find their symptoms fading away until they have cleared up completely. However, mistakes and mix-ups happen, and at some point, most gluten-sensitive people get "glutened"— they eat gluten by accident. This brings on symptoms fast and sometimes not even the same symptoms they were having before going gluten-free. Acid reflux is common, or someone who previously experienced diarrhea might end up constipated.

Doctors recommend various methods of recovering from getting glutened, but the usual advice is to drink a large amount of water. Flushing out the body's systems is the most effective way to get over gluten exposure quickly. Taking digestive enzymes and probiotics can also help by breaking down the gluten and balancing the gut microbiome. The ginger in ginger ale soothes upset stomachs, and over-the-counter pain medication can keep discomfort to a minimum while the body heals. It can take up to a week to recover from getting glutened, but with the proper care, celiac sufferers can quickly get on with their lives.

After getting glutened, drinking a lot of water is recommended to flush the body's systems as quickly as possible.

six to twelve months, a dietitian will go over these guidelines with their patient again and make sure they are sticking to the plan that has been laid out. This way, if the patient is confused about something or has become lazy in avoiding gluten, the dietitian can correct them before they do more damage to themselves.

Going on a Gluten-Free Diet

The most important thing for celiac patients to remember when going gluten-free is that a gluten-free diet looks very similar to a regular healthy diet. Rachel Begun, a culinary nutritionist and gluten-free diet expert, said that most meals should involve "naturally wholesome gluten-free foods, such as vegetables, fruits, beans, nuts, seeds, fish and lean meat,"[25] just like any balanced diet. Even grains, as long as they are gluten-free, are fine for celiac patients to eat. The problem comes when people going gluten-free begin depending on heavily processed foods such as prepackaged baked goods, frozen meals, or pizza. Junk food is junk food, gluten-free or not, so it should be eaten in moderation.

Although it may seem like there are not a lot of foods one can eat on a gluten-free diet, it is really an invitation to try new things. Wheat, rye, and barley are not the only grains out there; corn and rice are both gluten-free, and so are "amaranth, arrowroot, buckwheat (kasha), cassava, flax, millet, quinoa, sorghum, soy, tapioca, teff, polenta and fonio."[26] Wheat flour, too, can be replaced by "buckwheat flour, millet flour, almond flour, chickpea flour, amaranth flour, brown rice flour and coconut flour,"[27] as well as others. The only difference between these products and wheat products is that they need a little help from other ingredients to give them the soft, spongy texture gluten creates. Xanthan gum, guar gum, extra baking powder, extra yeast, and bananas are all common ingredients in gluten-free baking that help breads, muffins, cookies, and more bake up soft and fluffy.

Cross-contamination and sneaky sources of gluten are the two biggest enemies of a gluten-free diet. Oats, for example, are technically gluten-free, but they are often processed with the same machinery as products that contain gluten, making most oats a hazard for those with celiac. When it comes to eating gluten-free, it is best to start becoming comfortable with reading ingredients lists and asking questions. Due to the rising number of people with gluten sensitivity, most gluten-free foods in the supermarket are now clearly labeled, so anything that does not specifically say "gluten free" on the package should be thoroughly inspected before it is eaten. At a restaurant, even one with a gluten-free menu, celiac sufferers should ask their servers about things such as salad dressing or seasonings, many of which contain gluten but are still served on a "gluten-sensitive" menu. Overall, going gluten-free is a process, and it takes time to learn how to plan ahead and to become familiar with what is truly gluten-free and what is not. For people with celiac disease, though, taking the time to learn how to navigate the minefield of gluten will ultimately make their lives much better.

Dietary Supplements

Since a major effect of celiac is that the small intestine becomes less efficient at absorbing nutrients, a big part of managing celiac is making sure the body is getting the vitamins and

Different Blend Bakery

Opened in 2015 by pastry chef Jessica Smith, Different Blend Bakery in Schenect-ady, New York, is an entirely gluten-free establishment. During her freshman year at the Culinary Institute of America, Smith was diagnosed with celiac disease and spent most of her time in the Baking and Pastry Arts program surrounded by food she could not eat. This inspired her to begin experimenting in gluten-free baking with the goal of creating pastries that were as good as, if not better than, their glutenous counterparts. In a process of trial and error, she eventually created many gluten-free pastry and baked goods recipes. By opening Different Blend, she not only had a chance to share her food with the world, she also gave gluten-free peo-ple a chance to live freely while in her bakery:

> I think it is necessary for people with gluten sensitivities to have a dedi-cated gluten free place to eat. The gluten free diet is one of involuntary restraint and limited options. Even when options are plentiful there is often second guessing about cross-contamination, an innocent oversight. A dedicated bakery or restaurant removes these hurdles and gives us an opportunity to feel normal and special at the same time. I love it when someone walks into the bakery and says, "I can eat anything here?!" It lets people feel special instead of feeling like the odd one out.[1]

1. Jessica Smith, interview by author, February 6, 2018.

minerals it needs. After diagnosing someone with celiac, doctors will generally have blood tests done to check their patient's nutrient levels. "People recently diagnosed with celiac disease are commonly deficient in fiber, iron, calcium, magnesium, zinc, folate, niacin, riboflavin, vitamin B12, and vitamin D, as well as in calories and protein. Deficiencies in copper and vitamin B6 are also pos-sible, but less common,"[28] according to the Celiac Disease Foundation. To combat nutrient loss, the doctor or a dietitian will prescribe a gluten-free multivitamin. A multivitamin also helps make up for the nutrient deficiencies in a lot of gluten-free foods, which are often not fortified with the same vitamins and minerals as wheat products.

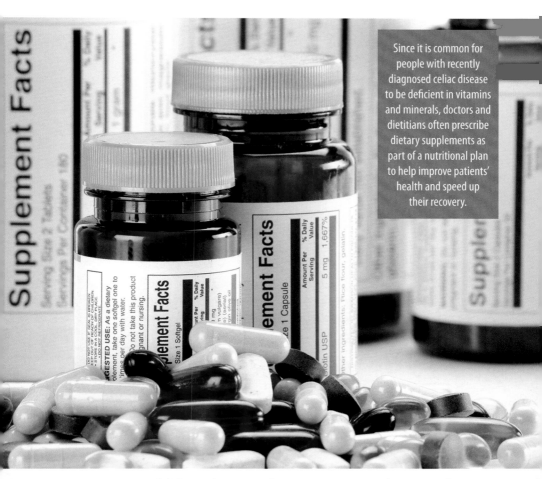

Since it is common for people with recently diagnosed celiac disease to be deficient in vitamins and minerals, doctors and dietitians often prescribe dietary supplements as part of a nutritional plan to help improve patients' health and speed up their recovery.

Although most dietitians agree that it is best to get key nutrients from food, they will generally prescribe dietary supplements to celiac patients to make sure they are getting the exact amount of nutrition they need. Calcium, vitamins D and B12, zinc, and magnesium are among the most commonly taken supplements by celiac sufferers. There can be too much of a good thing, however, so it is important that they take only the amount prescribed and avoid overdosing. Eventually, after a year or so of a strict gluten-free diet, the small intestine will begin to recover. With their dietitian's permission, celiac patients may not have to rely so heavily on supplements after a few years of successfully managing their disease.

Home Remedies

The only true treatment for celiac disease is a lifelong gluten-free diet, but there are some natural ways to treat celiac symptoms and speed the body's recovery from damage done by the immune system. Keeping the digestive system balanced is the best thing a celiac patient can do, so anti-inflammatory agents and probiotics are both recommended. However, some probiotics may contain gluten, so as with other foods, it is important for people with celiac to do research before trying one. Aloe vera, paprika, and ginger are all well-known anti-inflammatories and can be taken in pill form or used in cooking.

Choosing a diet that is free of gluten, cooking with anti-inflammatory spices such as paprika and ginger, and eating probiotic yogurt to increase intestinal flora are all actions that can help keep a celiac patient's digestive system balanced.

Probiotics, particularly those containing *Lactobacillus*, help reestablish good bacteria in the gut microbiome, which in turn can help the body break down gluten faster if it is accidentally eaten. Another natural supplement that may help is glutamine, "an amino acid that helps maintain intestinal metabolism and function and seems to benefit patients who have had intestinal injury from serious insults such as chemotherapy and radiation,"[29] according to Dr. Andrew Weil. Of course, celiac patients should talk to their doctor or dietitian before adding supplements to their diet, but trying something simple such as a probiotic yogurt may make a surprisingly large difference in how they feel.

An entire anti-inflammatory diet may also help those with celiac disease. Basically, an anti-inflammatory diet involves foods that "any mainstream nutrition expert would encourage you to eat. They include lots of fruits and vegetables … plant-based proteins (like beans and nuts), fatty fish, and fresh herbs and spices."[30] For people without celiac disease, this diet would also include whole grains. Foods to avoid would be things that are "highly processed, overly greasy, or super sweet,"[31] such as high-fat dairy products, fried food, or anything with trans fats. This kind of diet is specifically designed to help people with inflammatory conditions, so celiac patients may benefit greatly from monitoring their diet for things other than gluten.

Finding Support

Mental health issues such as depression and anxiety can be symptoms of celiac disease, but they can also arise after getting a celiac diagnosis. With significant life changes, such as having to go

Support groups can help newly diagnosed celiac sufferers cope with the significant life change a celiac diagnosis brings and can teach them how to live gluten-free in a gluten-rich world, even when eating out.

gluten-free, there is always a chance that a mental health problem will arise from the stress and worry. Frustration with watching one's diet, fear of getting glutened, and feeling like an outsider because of dietary restrictions are all common responses when celiac patients first begin getting accustomed to their new way of life. These feelings can lead people to give up on their gluten-free diet, especially when they feel hopeless or scared, but falling off the gluten-free wagon only does more internal damage, makes symptoms worse, and starts the cycle over again. Celiac sufferers are encouraged to talk to someone if they begin to feel sad or lonely, even if that someone is just a close relative or friend. They can talk to a therapist or a counselor, too, if they feel they need professional help.

To combat feelings of loneliness and confusion, celiac experts also encourage newly diagnosed patients to join support groups. These groups may simply be local gatherings, they may be connected to a larger system of support such as the Gluten Intolerance Group, or they may be online. The resources they provide are invaluable. "Many support groups provide information about celiac disease that your doctor may not give you," wrote Marie Suszynski of Everyday Health, "and you'll be surrounded by people who can guide you through living with celiac disease."[32] Being able to ask questions of people who have been gluten-free for years can help put new celiac patients' minds to rest. Going to a restaurant with a support group and observing how more experienced gluten-free eaters order can lessen fear about getting glutened when eating out.

Making friends with other people in similar situations can make the hard parts of celiac a little easier and has been proven to successfully keep people on their gluten-free diets. Knowing they are not alone is one of the most important things for anyone who has been diagnosed with a serious disease, and celiac is no exception.

Cutting Out FODMAPs

Evidence suggests that many cases of non-celiac gluten sensitivity may actually be FODMAP sensitivity, so doctors have begun to recommend low-FODMAP diets to NCGS sufferers. Originally created for patients with irritable bowel syndrome (IBS), a low-FODMAP diet is similar to a gluten-free diet because they both exclude wheat, rye, barley, and triticale, but they are different in an important way. Unlike gluten, which is found only in certain grains, FODMAPs are short chain carbohydrates, or sugars, that are found in many kinds of foods. In an article for the website Healthline, Dr. Megan Rossi broke down the four groups of FODMAPs:

- *Oligosaccharides: Wheat, rye, legumes and various fruits and vegetables, such as garlic and onions.*

- *Disaccharides: Milk, yogurt and soft cheese. Lactose is the main carb.*

- *Monosaccharides: Various fruit including figs and mangoes, and sweeteners such as honey and agave nectar. Fructose is the main carb.*

- *Polyols: Certain fruits and vegetables including blackberries and lychee, as well as some low-calorie sweeteners like those in sugar-free gum.*[33]

It may also benefit celiac patients to look more closely at FODMAPs. While FODMAP intolerance is not part of celiac disease, some people have what is known as "poorly responsive" celiac, meaning that their symptoms do not go away even after they adopt a gluten-free diet. Poorly responsive celiac is generally the result of continued gluten ingestion, whether by accident or on purpose, but it can also be a sign of some other inflammatory bowel disorder such as microscopic colitis, Crohn's disease, or ulcerative colitis. Lactose or fructose intolerance are also possible factors, along with IBS, all of which have shown improvement with a low-FODMAP diet. The Celiac Disease Foundation stated that a low-FODMAP diet is "most effective under the guidance of a skilled, experienced dietitian, who will systematically help you eliminate and reintroduce different categories of the FODMAPs,"[34] so it is best not to cut every source of FODMAPs from one's diet all at once, otherwise it will be difficult to tell which FODMAP is the true culprit. Keeping a balance but seeing improvements is key.

CHAPTER FOUR

MYTHS AND MISCONCEPTIONS

Even with the incidence of celiac disease rising from 0.2 percent to 1 percent of the American population since the 1950s, as well as the media explosion surrounding the gluten-free diet over the last decade, both celiac disease and gluten remain a mystery to a lot of people. Not only are scientists and doctors still working to crack celiac's code, but most people who have never had to deal with gluten sensitivity in themselves or their families know woefully little about the disease. This leads to the spread of misinformation—for instance, the idea that celiac is not a serious disease or that the gluten-free diet is only a fad. Misunderstandings such as these can be harmful to people with celiac disease, not only making their condition a topic of debate but also, in some cases, preventing them from getting the help they need.

Misinformation about gluten is also causing an opposite reaction to the dismissal that many celiac patients are used to; some people take the rise in celiac as a sign that gluten is bad for everyone and go on a gluten-free diet unnecessarily. These people often report miraculous improvements in their health after going gluten-free, but nutritionists believe this is either simply a result of them eating healthier in general because of the restrictions of a gluten-free diet or a sign that they had an undiagnosed gluten sensitivity to begin with. The problem with going gluten-free without having a medical reason is that, by nature, a gluten-free diet is unbalanced, making it an unhealthy decision in the long run if done incorrectly. To keep everyone healthy, medical experts and the media are working to educate the masses on the truth about celiac and gluten to minimize the spread of myths.

Celiac Is a Serious Disease

One of the most common misconceptions about celiac is that it is not very serious, but that is far from the truth. While it is true that most of the damage done inside the body by the immune system will eventually be repaired after going on a gluten-free diet, the consequences of leaving celiac disease untreated can be lifelong and devastating. "Left untreated, celiac disease increases a person's risk of developing thyroid disorders, severe infections, certain kinds of cardiovascular disease, neurological problems such as numbness and tingling in the hands and feet, or osteoporosis,"[35] according to the *U.S. News & World Report*. Infertility, miscarriage, and cancers of the white blood cells and small intestine are also very real possibilities if celiac goes undiagnosed. Unfortunately, many cases of celiac disease are only found once these other serious problems, which are more difficult to treat than celiac, are discovered. Finding more efficient ways of diagnosing celiac is important to save patients a great deal of unnecessary pain and suffering.

Other side effects of celiac, such as vitamin and mineral deficiency, anemia, lactose intolerance, and even low bone density, can be reversed by a gluten-free diet and dietary supplements, but that does not make them less serious. If left for long

Undiagnosed celiac disease can wreak havoc on the immune system over time, making it difficult for sufferers to fight off illness and infection.

enough, these disorders can make a person weak and unable to fight off illnesses and infections, which is especially dangerous for children and the elderly. Even though celiac seems like only an inconvenience on the surface, it has major repercussions. All too often, celiac patients take their diagnosis too lightly and do not stick to a gluten-free diet the way they should. Eventually, they end up with much more serious issues than diarrhea and bloating.

Going Gluten-Free Is Not a Fad

One of the most pervasive myths about the gluten-free diet is that it is a fad diet that will fall

Leaky Gut

Increased intestinal permeability, or "leaky gut," is one of the side effects of the inflammation in the small intestine caused by celiac. According to a website maintained by Dr. Andrew Weil, leaky gut is understood this way:

> Damage to the intestinal lining can also make the gut less able to protect the internal environment, and disrupt its ability to filter nutrients and other biological substances that pass through it. This can potentially allow certain bacteria and their toxins, as well as incompletely digested proteins and fats, and waste not normally absorbed to "leak" from the intestines into the blood stream. This process can trigger additional immune responses, thus worsening symptoms and contributing to the cycle of intestinal discomfort.[1]

Although all celiac patients are likely to have some degree of leaky gut, doctors rarely talk about it. Very little research has gone into studying it, and it is assumed to go away once the intestines begin to heal after a patient starts a gluten-free diet. It is, however, a serious risk for undiagnosed celiac sufferers since it exposes them to infections.

1. Andrew Weil, "Celiac Disease Symptoms and Treatment," Dr. Weil, accessed on December 21, 2017. www.drweil.com/health-wellness/body-mind-spirit/gastrointestinal/celiac-disease/.

out of popularity in a few years. This, of course, does not take into account the thousands of people who have to be on gluten-free diets because of celiac disease or NCGS. However, because the gluten-free diet has gone mainstream and is being practiced by people who do not need to be on it, anyone who says they need gluten-free food may instantly be assumed to be one of those people. In a blog post about the consequences of the gluten-free craze, the National Wheat Foundation pointed out that

> the 30 percent of the American population "trying to avoid gluten" are creating a stigma that anyone asking for "gluten-free" meal options is simply on the fad-diet bandwagon. Those with celiac disease are finding that this diet trend

is leading to servers passing judgment or not following necessary precautions when they ask for dietary menu requests.[36]

This is a major source of stress for celiac patients. Getting glutened at a restaurant is a painful experience, and it can be discouraging to newly diagnosed celiac sufferers who are just starting to feel better after years of struggling with the disease.

Because some servers dismiss those who request a gluten-free option as fad dieters, celiac sufferers must be careful when eating out.

On the other hand, it would be incorrect to say that there is not a little bit of truth behind this myth. In the past decade, the number of people on a gluten-free diet in the United States has skyrocketed while the rate of celiac disease has remained constant. "Gluten is to this decade what carbohydrates were to the last one and fat was to the '80s and '90s," said Jeffrey Kluger of *TIME* magazine, "the bête noir, the bad boy, the cause of all that ails you—and the elimination of which can heal you."[37] However, even those without celiac disease who feel better on a gluten-free diet deserve respect. NCGS is still unknown territory in the medical community, so it is difficult to tell how many people who avoid gluten are actually benefiting from it and how many are experiencing a placebo effect, which means the person only thinks they feel better because they have been told they will feel better. Either way, making assumptions about people based on their diet does not help anyone; it only hurts people with serious medical conditions.

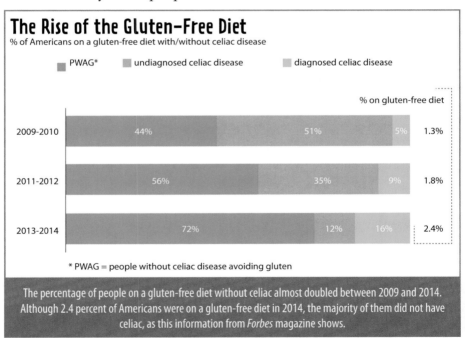

The Rise of the Gluten-Free Diet
% of Americans on a gluten-free diet with/without celiac disease

■ PWAG*   ■ undiagnosed celiac disease   ■ diagnosed celiac disease

% on gluten-free diet

				% on gluten-free diet
2009-2010	44%	51%	5%	1.3%
2011-2012	56%	35%	9%	1.8%
2013-2014	72%	12%	16%	2.4%

* PWAG = people without celiac disease avoiding gluten

The percentage of people on a gluten-free diet without celiac almost doubled between 2009 and 2014. Although 2.4 percent of Americans were on a gluten-free diet in 2014, the majority of them did not have celiac, as this information from *Forbes* magazine shows.

Gluten Is Not Bad for Everyone
There is, however, a subgroup of people on gluten-free diets who are legitimately uninformed and following bad advice from unqualified sources.

These people believe gluten increases "the risk of obesity, cardiovascular disease, psychiatric problems and metabolic issues,"[38] even though no medical research has backed up these claims. While obesity and heart disease are serious issues in America, they are directly associated with the lack of nutritional value found in the average American diet. Gluten, while not particularly nutritious by itself, is found primarily in grains, and whole grains are an important part of good nutrition. In fact, whole grains have been proven to reduce the risk of heart disease, so claiming that they cause cardiovascular problems is simply untrue. Furthermore, the fatigue, headaches, "brain fog," depression, anxiety, and digestive problems some people claim are cured by a gluten-free diet are all symptoms of both celiac and NCGS, which means they most likely have a gluten-related disorder. This has nothing to do, then, with gluten, but has everything to do with how these individuals process it. It is faulty logic to assume that just because gluten is bad for some people, it is bad for everyone.

The bad logic of the gluten-free trend started in 2011, when a cardiologist—a doctor who specializes in heart problems—named Dr. William Davis published his book *Wheat Belly*, which claimed that the secret to weight loss and a healthy life is removing wheat from the diet. His assumption was based on an informal study he conducted on himself and his friends, which in the world of scientific investigation is not considered a real experiment. As a weight loss plan, it caught on because the diet he proposed is relatively healthy aside from the exclusion of whole grains. It cuts out "high-fructose corn syrup, sucrose, salt, sugary foods, rice, potatoes, soda, fruit juice, dried fruit, legumes … trans fats, fried foods, and cured meats,"[39] most of

Brain Fog

Among the neurological problems caused by gluten sensitivity is what is known as "brain fog," a feeling of tiredness that lasts all day. While not officially medically recognized as a symptom of celiac and other autoimmune disorders, brain fog is a very real phenomenon generally associated with fibromyalgia and chronic fatigue syndrome. Signs of brain fog include:

- Difficulty concentrating

- Problems with attentiveness

- Lapses in short-term memory

- Difficulty finding the right words while speaking or writing

- Forgetfulness

- Temporary loss of mental acuity and creativity

- Confusion or disorientation[1]

Among celiac sufferers, brain fog is often not registered as a symptom until after beginning a gluten-free diet, when the fog finally lifts and they can concentrate for the first time in their lives. However, very little research has been done on brain fog, and doctors remain unsure what exactly causes it.

It is often not until celiac disease is diagnosed and the patient is on a gluten-free diet that they realize how much the disease affected their ability to think clearly.

1. Andrew Weil, "Celiac Disease Symptoms and Treatment," Dr. Weil, accessed on December 21, 2017. www.drweil.com/health-wellness/body-mind-spirit/gastrointestinal/celiac-disease/.

which would be cut out when going on a regular healthy diet. Since then, celebrities such as Victoria Beckham, Gwyneth Paltrow, and Miley Cyrus have jumped on the bandwagon, influencing others to go gluten-free for no reason.

Celiac Is Not a Wheat Allergy

There are many types of medical conditions that are triggered by the consumption of gluten or wheat, but each is unique and requires different treatments. People often mistake celiac for an allergy to wheat or gluten, but allergies and autoimmune disorders are separate conditions.

"An allergy," wrote food blogger and celiac advocate Rebecca on her blog, "is when a specific food is ingested that triggers a severe immune response by the body, mistaking the food as a harmful invader like a virus or bacteria ... An autoimmune disease is when your immune system attacks your own healthy body cells, damaging the cells, tissues, and organs."[40] Unlike celiac and NCGS, a wheat allergy is a bodily response to more than just

Although people sometimes confuse celiac symptoms for an allergic reaction, allergies and autoimmune disorders are entirely separate conditions.

the gluten protein—wheat itself is the problem. It is also much easier to treat an allergy. Sneezing, coughing, itching, and hives can generally be treated with an over-the-counter antihistamine, and even a more severe reaction such as anaphylaxis, which causes difficulty breathing and facial swelling, can be treated with an EpiPen.

Dermatitis herpetiformis, the "gluten rash," sometimes occurs as a symptom of celiac disease, but it can also occur alone as a reaction to gluten. The rash is the result of an immune reaction such as celiac and is a sign of the body attacking itself. Even if someone tests negative for celiac, they may

A rash can occur as an allergic reaction to gluten even when celiac disease or NCGS is not present.

have to avoid gluten anyway to keep the rash from returning after taking an antibiotic to clear it.

Another immune reaction to gluten is called gluten ataxia, where antibodies attack the brain rather than the small intestine. In particular, they attack the cerebellum, which controls motor function. "This damage potentially can cause problems with your gait [walk] and with your gross motor skills, resulting in loss of coordination and possibly leading to significant, progressive disability in some cases,"[41] wrote Jane Anderson of Verywell. Ataxia is rare—only about 8 out of 100,000 Americans develop some form of it—so gluten ataxia is even rarer. However, it is important to remember that it has nothing to do with celiac disease aside from having the same trigger.

Breastfeeding Cannot Prevent Celiac

For a long time—up until 2015—doctors told new mothers that breastfeeding their babies for as long as possible would delay or even prevent the onset of celiac disease. This seemed to make sense; breastfeeding has been proven to protect babies from food allergies, type 1 diabetes, multiple sclerosis, and many other illnesses because it passes important immune cells from mother to child and builds up the infant's immune system. In 2006, "an analysis by a group in England who reviewed all the papers published at the time that had to do with the protective role of breastfeeding and celiac disease concluded that there is a significant protective role," Dr. Stefano Guandalini said in an interview with *Science Life*. "There were two components to it. One was the duration of breastfeeding: the longer the better, up to a year. The second component was having a baby breastfed at the time of gluten introduction."[42]

In 2015, however, two European studies dis-proved this theory. In one, 553 newborns from families with a history of celiac disease were given gluten at different times during their first year—either at six months like most babies, or later, at twelve months—and then followed for 10 years to see if they would develop celiac and, if they did, at what age it happened. In the end, the prevalence of the disease was the same in both groups.

Although breastfeeding can be good for an infant's health and well-being, studies show that it does not prevent celiac disease.

In the second study, more than 1,000 infants were observed. "The intervention this time was different," Guandalini said. "The idea was that giving small amounts of gluten between four and six months would be preventative because most babies at this age were still being breastfed and it would induce tolerance."[43] As with the other children, over time, the rate of developing celiac was no lower for these children who were introduced to gluten while still breastfeeding. These findings surprised the medical community, but no one could deny that the studies were better than any before them. Now doctors have to fight to retract their previous assumptions about breastfeeding and celiac from the public eye and educate new mothers with up-to-date research.

Celiac Does Not Make Life Miserable

After first receiving their celiac diagnosis, most patients take it the way one would expect: not well. Having to shift one's life around completely to accommodate a new, unwanted gluten-free diet is saddening and stressful. No one wants to give up food they love, but regular pasta, pizza, and many other favorites all go on the chopping block when celiac moves in. No one wants to be the inconvenient one, either—the person who has to get a special menu, who does not eat at parties, or who has to buy expensive versions of everyday grocery items such as bread and cereal. These are all concerns for the newly diagnosed celiac patient, but they have to power through them to avoid facing the health consequences.

However, just because a gluten-free life is hard sometimes does not mean it has to be miserable. "I can choose to find the good, the happy and the positive in my everyday life,"[44] wrote Kristin, a food blogger who was diagnosed with celiac after the birth of her son. Ultimately, after learning the ins and outs of navigating their disease, celiac patients live long, healthy lives and are no more unhappy than the average person. In an article for Gluten Free Therapeutics, an anonymous writer came to this conclusion:

> *We found the key is to be proactive, stick up for one's self, learn and always plan ahead. Knowing the key to our good health is a gluten free diet is empowering because we are in control. There are no drugs with side effects needed. If we stay completely gluten free our health rebounds and we feel terrific. It can take time to negotiate the social landmines we face but we can do it. And it feels great!*[45]

CHAPTER FIVE

TAKING THE NEXT STEP

Because of the restrictive nature of a gluten-free diet, scientists are currently racing to be the first to find an effective medical treatment for celiac. There are so many options for methods of treatment—including enzymes, antibodies, immunotherapy, molecule inhibitors, vaccination, and others—that it is difficult to say who will win the race, but it is possible it could be won sometime in the next decade. However, finding a treatment or a cure that works is not the only problem scientists are required to solve. "Any novel [new] medication for celiac disease should be as effective and safe as the gluten-free diet,"[46] a panel of experts said after reviewing the progress of celiac treatments in 2012. So not only does a treatment need to work, it needs to have as few side effects as simply cutting out gluten. If it does not, there is no benefit to having it.

In June 2017, four celiac treatments were in Phase 2 clinical trials. This means they were being tested on 100 to 300 patients with celiac disease to see if they actually worked. They were already deemed safe in Phase 1, which is done on a smaller group of volunteers, but for a treatment to move up to Phase 3, it must be proven to have a positive effect on the disease it is trying to treat. Any serious doubt of a drug's effectiveness will send it back to the preclinical phase, where it will be reformulated and tested for safety in a Phase 1 trial again. This is often where new medications and treatments get stuck, but hopefully, soon one will break the cycle. Until then, however, it is possible that any treatment method could be the one to treat or cure celiac for good.

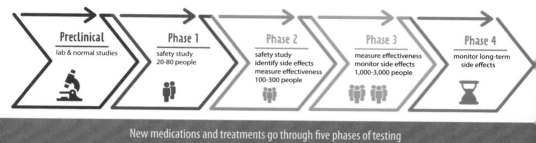

Preclinical
lab & normal studies

Phase 1
safety study
20-80 people

Phase 2
safety study
identify side effects
measure effectiveness
100-300 people

Phase 3
measure effectiveness
monitor side effects
1,000-3,000 people

Phase 4
monitor long-term
side effects

New medications and treatments go through five phases of testing to make sure they are safe and effective for humans.

Enzymes

Enzymes are proteins that break things down, and in each of the three enzyme treatments currently being developed for celiac, the goal is to break down gluten. From the current research, it does not seem that enzymes could replace a gluten-free diet but would instead work alongside a gluten-free diet to prevent people from getting glutened. In an interview with the National Foundation for Celiac Awareness, Dr. David Leffler had this to say about the uses of enzymes for celiac disease:

> There are some people who are either high-ly sensitive to gluten or have diets that are difficult to fully control, for instance college students on a meal plan or frequent business travelers. For these individuals, this type of a medication would be most effective if taken routinely. On the other hand, there are people who can achieve adequate dietary control most of the time, but will need some extra protection

on weekends when they eat out or on vacation, for example.[47]

While this is clearly not a method that will remove the risk of gluten, it could reduce it significantly enough that people with celiac disease could relax when eating at a restaurant or a friend's house and not have to worry about becoming sick after being glutened. This alone would be revolutionary.

Enzyme therapy could help celiac patients such as college students avoid getting glutened in situations where they have less control over the type of food they have access to.

As of June 2017, two enzyme treatments are at different stages of clinical trials. KumaMax, which is being developed by the start-up company PvP Biologics, is in the preclinical phase, while latiglutenase, or IMGX003, is in Phase 2 trials at a lab called ImmunogenX. A third enzyme, called AN-PEP, is available in the United States as a dietary supplement called GliadinX. It has not undergone testing and approval by the U.S. Food and Drug Administration (FDA), but independent tests have shown that it can help reduce the effects of getting glutened in people with NCGS. Taken with a meal, each of these enzymes has shown, to some extent, the ability to break down gluten before it reaches the small intestine and causes an immune reaction. Unfortunately, none of them have proven to break down all of the gluten in a meal, so they are currently being promoted as supplements to a gluten-free diet for celiac patients in the case of accidental gluten exposure. Julia König, one of the researchers who tested AN-PEP, noted that the research team cannot be certain the enzyme breaks down every bit of gluten, so eating gluten could still do long-term harm to someone with celiac disease even if they take the supplement. However, for people with mild NCGS, enzymes may be an easy fix for their symptoms, allowing them to avoid a gluten-free diet altogether.

Antibodies

During an immune reaction, white blood cells produce antibodies to fight off the gluten they believe is a foreign invader. To communicate, one cell to the next, they also produce cytokines, which are molecules that transfer information. In the GI tract, a particular cytokine called interleukin-15 (IL-15) is crucial to the mass movement of immune cells toward gluten molecules. As of late 2017, three kinds of antibodies have been modified to specifically target IL-15 and block the immune response by preventing immune cells from "talking" to each other. CALY-002 from Calypso Biotech, a biopharmaceutical company, is in preclinical trials. Hu-Mik-Beta 1, a collaborative effort from the

National Cancer Institute and the Mayo Clinic, is in Phase 1. Finally, AMG 714 from a company called Celimmune is in Phase 2.

Another possible use of modified antibodies would be to neutralize the white blood cells, or T-cells, themselves. To activate and begin an immune response, T-cells must receive certain molecules that fit into receptors on their surface like a key into a lock. One of these receptors, OX40, is responsible for a variety of autoimmune diseases, including rheumatoid arthritis, multiple sclerosis, IBS, atopic dermatitis, and celiac disease. Glenmark Pharmaceuticals' antibody, GBR 830, is called an OX40 antagonist, meaning that it attacks the OX40 receptor on white blood cells to prevent

There are many ways for medications and other medical treatments to enter the body. Injections are one common way; another is a pill.

Refractory Celiac

In some rare cases, a person's celiac disease may not respond to a gluten-free diet, even if no gluten is being eaten at all and there is no other GI issue. This is called refractory celiac disease, or RCD, and about 1.5 percent of celiac patients develop it. "People with true refractory celiac disease … are at much higher risk for serious complications, including a form of non-Hodgkin lymphoma associated with celiac disease,"[1] reported Jane Anderson of Verywell.

If someone's celiac does not improve over the course of a year or so after diagnosis, their doctor will begin the process of ruling out causes. First, they may check to make sure that the patient has not been misdiagnosed with celiac, and they will perform the diagnostic tests again. If the tests come back positive for celiac, then the second question is whether the patient has been adhering to a strict gluten-free diet. The doctor will reeducate the patient on how to avoid gluten, or they will refer them to a dietitian if they do not have one already. If the patient is truly not eating any gluten, then the doctor will diagnose them with refractory celiac disease. The patient will then most likely be sent to a specialist who will try various methods to induce intestinal healing.

When testing for refractory celiac, the doctor may discover that the patient simply needs extra instruction in how to maintain a healthy, gluten-free diet.

1. Jane Anderson, "What Is Refractory Celiac Disease?," Verywell, December 14, 2017. www.Verywell.com/what-is-refractory-celiac-disease-563003.

activation. As of early 2018, only Phase 1 trials were complete to test GBR 830's effectiveness on atopic dermatitis, but celiac tests may be on the horizon. This, as well as the other antibody methods, may be best used to treat refractory celiac disease, which does not respond to a gluten-free diet.

Vaccinations

When it comes to celiac, one's own immune system is the biggest enemy. With this in mind, labs are working on vaccinations that can change how the immune system responds to gluten. One is Selecta Biosciences with its as-yet-unnamed synthetic vaccine particles, or SVPs. SVPs are "designed to program the immune system to elicit tolerance to a specific antigen without impacting the rest of the immune system."[48] They prevent the formation of antibodies specific to a certain invader—in celiac's case, gluten—by teaching the T-cells to ignore it. Both SVP-wrapped rapamycin, a "teacher" molecule, and SVP-wrapped gliadin, the major protein in gluten that triggers an immune response, are injected into a subject and inform the immune cells not to react to the gliadin. In the future, the immune cells will remember this particular instruction and will not react. This is in contrast to immunosuppression drugs; these keep the immune system from reacting to any invader, including gluten, but this means the immune system does not work as it was designed to. People who are on these drugs have a much higher risk of getting sick, and their illnesses are harder to treat.

Although the process sounds fancy, it is, in fact, how other potential vaccines work as well: A guardian agent escorts gluten proteins through the body, teaching the immune system along the way

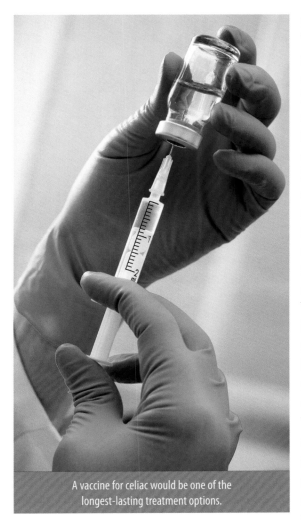

A vaccine for celiac would be one of the longest-lasting treatment options.

to tolerate them. TIMP-GLIA is the name of a vaccine from Cour Pharmaceuticals, and Nexvax2 is the name of a vaccine from ImmusanT. The main difference between these three vaccines is where the immune system is taught. With Selecta Biosciences SVPs, the lymph nodes learn and pass the information to the T-cells. With TIMP-GLIA, the spleen learns and passes the information to the T-cells. With Nexvax2, the T-cells themselves are targeted and learn directly from the vaccine. Nexvax2 is the kind of treatment that would need a booster shot every few years to retrain the immune system, and like the enzyme method, it would have to be used alongside a gluten-free diet. It would, however, protect celiac patients from small amounts of gluten for an extended period of time, meaning their gluten-free diet might not have to be so strict.

Inhibitors

Another way to treat disease is to inhibit, or prevent, certain functions that allow the disease to happen. One type of medical inhibitor is a gene inhibitor, which is what Provid Pharmaceuticals has in the preclinical phase as of early 2018. Currently nameless, its two gene inhibitors are directed at HLA-DQ2 and HLA-DQ8, the genes responsible for celiac disease. Although very little has been revealed about them, the inhibitors will probably work the same way most do: by turning off DQ2 and DQ8 or preventing them from being turned on in the first place. This method is called silencing genes, and it occurs through a process called RNA interference:

> Messenger RNA, or mRNA, carries a gene's instructions to structures in a cell known as ribosomes (ry-boh-sohmz). This information tells other RNA molecules in those ribosomes to make some particular protein. Those proteins will carry out most of a cell's functions.
>
> But not every cell needs to do every task. For example, nerve cells and skin cells have very different tasks. Nor must each cell work at the same time. Instead, each cell expresses—or turns on—the genes that it needs for a particular job at some particular time. Different RNA molecules help control that process.[49]

Using different proteins, RNA cuts through mRNA and prevents it from delivering its message to the ribosomes to make certain proteins. In the case of celiac disease, turning off DQ2 and DQ8 would keep the cells in the small intestine from triggering an autoimmune response.

Enzyme inhibitors for TG2 are another option. TG2 is the enzyme that reacts with gliadin and makes it more attracted to sensitive immune cells in the small intestine, causing the inflammation and destruction of the villi that make celiac so serious. Two biotech companies, Sitari Pharma and Zedira, are both developing enzyme inhibitors to prevent the chemical reaction between TG2 and gliadin, thereby minimizing the reaction between gliadin and the immune system. Like other methods of treatment, this one would involve a mostly gluten-free diet, but it would also allow some dietary freedom for celiac patients.

Larazotide Acetate

Leaky gut, or increased intestinal permeability, is a side effect of celiac disease that has been inexplicably left without much research into it. Perhaps this is because it is assumed to be a given or a matter of logic when it comes to the damage of the body: If tissue gets damaged, it becomes weaker and can allow foreign particles to infiltrate it. This is known to be true with open wounds on the skin, and people cover them up with bandages to prevent foreign particles from getting in and causing an infection. In the small intestine, increased permeability has been attributed to the weakening of something called tight junctions. In a 2008 interview, Dr. David Leffler defined tight junctions in a conversation about leaky gut:

> *The cells lining the intestine are linked together by a complex of proteins known as "tight junctions." These exist throughout the entire intestinal tract but cells are bound more tightly together in some areas.*

> *These barriers are important ways that your body regulates what comes in and out of the intestinal lining. It has been*

suggested that if these tight junctions are not working well, proteins and even microorganisms might be able to get into the body past the intestinal lining causing disease or symptoms.[50]

Repeated inflammations are known to weaken tight junctions between cells, and celiac is a disease of repeated inflammations. This leaves the intestine with no defense against future gluten, allowing more inflammation and further damage to the villi.

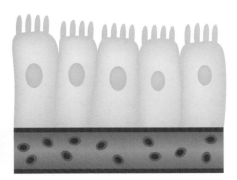
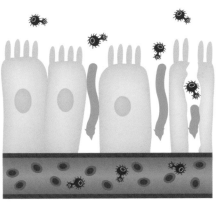

normal tight junction   **leaky and inflamed**

Gaps between the cells of the small intestine allow foreign particles such as gluten through the barrier and into the bloodstream.

Larazotide acetate, or INN-202, is a synthetic peptide that has proven to regulate tight junctions in Phase 2 clinical trials. "Early research suggests larazotide acetate helps to keep the tight junctions closed when it's taken before a meal, thus reducing or stopping the domino effects of inflammation,"[51] reported *Allergic Living* after INN-202 finished Phase 2 trials in 2016. Innovate Biopharmaceuticals received fast track designation from the FDA, meaning it had permission to complete its trials more quickly, but Phase 3 clinical trials were pushed off until 2018. It was the only drug for celiac disease headed for Phase 3 trials at that time, making it a likely candidate for winner of the celiac treatment race.

The Party City Ad

In January 2018, Party City ran a Super Bowl advertisement that got quite a bit of negative attention from the celiac community. *People* magazine reported,

> The ad features two people in a room decorated and ready for a Super Bowl party. A large snack table is on display and to the right of it is a single plate of food separated on a stool.
>
> "Those are some gluten-free options," one woman says in the commercial.
>
> "Do we even know people that are like that?" another woman asked.
>
> "Tina," the first woman responded.
>
> "Oh, gross, yeah," the second woman said.[1]

As soon as the ad aired, people on Twitter vented their anger in Party City's direction. "As a parent to a child with celiac disease I am disgusted,"[2] a mother said, and someone else commented, "PPL [people] choose to eat GF [gluten-free] for many reasons, none of which should be mocked or scorned."[3] "My celiac disease is not your punchline,"[4] one Twitter user told Party City in no uncertain terms. Since then, Party City has removed the ad from TV and YouTube and has apologized for hurting the gluten-free community, even going so far as making a donation toward celiac research.

1. Alexia Fernandez, "Party City Apologizes and Pulls Ad After Offending People with Gluten Allergies," *People*, January 23, 2018. people.com/food/party-city-apologizes-for-offending-gluten-free-people-after-commercial-called-them-gross/.

2. Courtney, Twitter post, January 22, 2018, 1:34pm. twitter.com/cmarkus99.

3. Kelly KillornMoravec, Twitter post, January 22, 2018, 2:23pm. twitter.com/KellyKillorn.

4. Sewprickly, Twitter post, January 22, 2018, 2:21pm. twitter.com/sewprickly.

How to Move Forward

Even though finding a treatment or a cure for celiac disease is guaranteed to improve life for celiac patients, that does not mean improving their lives should be put on hold until that happens. Even someone who is not personally affected by celiac or NCGS can make an effort to advocate for the celiac community as a way to show support. Getting better gluten-free meals into schools, defining the standards of gluten-free menus in restaurants, and just being taken seriously in general are all battles celiac sufferers are still fighting. Since they are a minority in the population, however, sometimes their voices are not heard, so it is everyone's job to speak up, magnify the message, and help make the changes that need to be made.

People can also help celiac patients just by being nice to them. Because of the current diet trend, the gluten-free community has become the target of bullying and unkind jokes for being "high-maintenance" or "alarmists," even though many gluten-free people do not want to choose the lifestyle. Making fun of people, especially about something they cannot change, is rude and does nothing but make them feel worse about something they may not be happy about in the first place.

If a friend or family member suspects that they might have celiac disease, being there for them is important. Learning about the condition, making changes around the house, and providing emotional support are all ways loved ones can make a big difference for someone dealing with a serious medical condition such as celiac, even before a diagnosis. "My first piece of advice would be to assure the person that this is a real condition and that they deserve to be taken seriously,"[52] said Suesana, a celiac sufferer who had symptoms for almost 35 years before being diagnosed in 2014. Being dismissed and having their pain downplayed by doctors, friends, and family is all too common for celiac patients, so listening to them and believing them about their symptoms is key. It may also help to suggest they keep a record of what they eat and what their symptoms are so they are prepared to talk to a doctor about their concerns. Ultimately, a celiac diagnosis is not the end of the world, but it requires determination and a strong support system to make the long journey back to good health.

NOTES

Introduction:
A Pain in the Gut

1. Jaclyn, "Jaclyn's Story," Celiac Answers, December 28, 2013. www.celiacanswers.com/jaclyns-story/#.WlT1mL9zLIU.

2. Adda Bjarnadottir, "What Is Gluten, and Why Is It Bad for Some People?," *Medical News Today*, June 3, 2017. www.medicalnewstoday.com/articles/318606.php.

Chapter One:
What Celiac Disease Does and How to Find It

3. "Celiac Disease Screening and Diagnosis," Celiac Disease Foundation, accessed on November 10, 2017. celiac.org/celiac-disease/understanding-celiac-disease-2/diagnosing-celiac-disease/.

4. Jaclyn, "Jaclyn's Story."

5. "Celiac Disease Symptoms," Celiac Disease Foundation, accessed on November 10, 2017. celiac.org/celiac-disease/understanding-celiac-disease-2/celiacdiseasesymptoms/.

6. Jane Anderson, "What Does It Mean When You Have Silent Celiac Disease?," Verywell, June 6, 2017. www.Verywell.com/asymptomatic-or-silent-celiac-disease-563125.

7. "At What Age Should Children Get Tested for Celiac Disease?," University of Chicago Celiac Disease Center, June 2017. www.cureceliacdisease.org/faq/at-what-age-should-children-get-tested-for-celiac-disease/.

8. "Non-Celiac Wheat Sensitivity," Celiac Disease Foundation, accessed on November 13, 2017. celiac.org/celiac-disease/understanding-celiac-disease-2/non-celiac-gluten-sensitivity-2/.

9. "At What Age Should Children Get Tested for Celiac Disease?," University of Chicago Celiac Disease Center.

10. Quoted in Cameron Scott, "Is Non-Celiac Gluten Sensitivity a Real Thing?," Healthline, August 15, 2016. www.healthline.com/health-news/is-non-celiac-gluten-sensitivity-a-real-thing-041615#1.

Chapter Two:
Looking for a Cause

11. Sheila Crowe, "Genetic Testing for Celiac Disease," *New York Times*, January 13, 2010. consults.blogs.nytimes.com/2010/01/13/genetic-testing-for-celiac-disease/.

12. Amy Leger, "Genetic Testing Can Reveal Your Family's Chances of Developing Celiac Disease," *Gluten-Free Living*, June 23, 2015. www.glutenfreeliving.com/gluten-free/celiac-disease/genetic-testing-celiac-disease/.

13. Valentina Discepolo, "Are Viruses Causing Celiac Disease?," *The Forefront*, University of Chicago Medicine, September 3, 2014. www.uchicagomedicine.org/gastrointestinal-articles/are-viruses-causing-celiac-disease.

14. Discepolo, "Are Viruses Causing Celiac Disease?"

15. Andreas Beyerlein, Ewan Donnachie, and Anette-Gabriele Ziegler, "Infections in

Early Life and Development of Celiac Disease," *American Journal of Epidemiology*, vol. 186, no. 11 (2017): 1279. doi.org/10.1093/aje/kwx190.

16. "Celiac Disease Risk Linked to Absence of Bacteria in the Gut," Celiac Disease Foundation, February 3, 2014. celiac.org/blog/2014/02/celiac-disease-risk-linked-to-absence-of-bacteria-in-the-gut/.

17. Kristina Campbell, "Studying How Gluten Reacts with Bacteria in the Gut Helps Advance Treatments for Celiac Disease," *Gut Microbiota for Health*, February 15, 2017. www.gutmicrobiotaforhealth.com/en/studying-gluten-reacts-bacteria-gut-helps-advance-treatments-celiac-disease/.

18. Jane Anderson, "Can Stress Trigger Celiac Disease?," Verywell, January 6, 2018. www.Verywell.com/can-stress-trigger-celiac-disease-3973237.

19. Anderson, "Can Stress Trigger Celiac Disease?"

20. Jane Anderson, "Can Pregnancy Trigger Celiac Disease?," Verywell, October 27, 2016. www.Verywell.com/can-pregnancy-trigger-celiac-disease-562302.

21. "Gluten Sensitivity and FODMAPs," Gluten Intolerance Group, October 5, 2017. www.gluten.org/resources/health-wellness/gluten-sensitivity-and-fodmaps/.

Chapter Three:
Managing Celiac Disease

22. Quoted in "Celiac Rant: Where's My Follow-Up Care?," *Gluten Dude*, September 19,

2012. glutendude.com/celiac-rant/celiac-follow-up-care/.

23. "Celiac Disease Treatment and Follow Up," Celiac Disease Foundation, accessed on December 18, 2017. celiac.org/celiac-disease/understanding-celiac-disease-2/treating-celiac-disease/.

24. Pam Cureton, "When, Why and How to Consult a Dietitian," *Gluten-Free Living*, June 3, 2014. www.glutenfreeliving.com/gluten-free/resources-support/how-to-consult-a-dietitian/.

25. Jessica Migala, "Starting a Gluten-Free Diet: A Guide for Beginners," *EatingWell*, May 2016. www.eatingwell.com/article/288542/starting-a-gluten-free-diet-a-guide-for-beginners/.

26. "The Basic Gluten-Free Diet," *Gluten-Free Living*, September 28, 2017. www.glutenfreeliving.com/gluten-free-foods/diet/basic-diet/.

27. "The Basic Gluten-Free Diet," *Gluten-Free Living*.

28. "Vitamins & Supplements," Celiac Disease Foundation, accessed on December 21, 2017. celiac.org/live-gluten-free/glutenfreediet/vitamins-and-supplements/.

29. Andrew Weil, "Celiac Disease Symptoms and Treatment," Dr. Weil, accessed on December 21, 2017. www.drweil.com/health-wellness/body-mind-spirit/gastrointestinal/celiac-disease/.

30. Kathleen M. Zelman, ed., "Anti-Inflammatory Diet: Road to Good Health?," WebMD, January 16, 2017. www.webmd.com/diet/anti-inflammatory-diet-road-to-good-health#1.

31. Zelman, ed., "Anti-Inflammatory Diet."

32. Marie Suszynski, "Support Groups for Celiac Disease," *Everyday Health*, November 22, 2013. www.everydayhealth.com/celiac-disease/celiac-disease-support-groups.aspx.

33. Megan Rossi, "A Beginner's Guide to the Low-FODMAP Diet," Healthline, March 15, 2017. www.healthline.com/nutrition/low-fodmap-diet.

34. "Poorly Responsive Celiac Disease," Celiac Disease Foundation, accessed on December 22, 2017. celiac.org/celiac-disease/understanding-celiac-disease-2/poorly-responsive-celiac-disease/.

Chapter Four:
Myths and Misconceptions

35. Stacey Colino, "5 Myths About Celiac Disease," *U.S. News & World Report*, May 18, 2016. health.usnews.com/wellness/articles/2016-05-18/5-myths-about-celiac-disease.

36. "The Consequences of a Gluten-Free Diet Craze," National Wheat Foundation, accessed on January 8, 2018. wheatfoundation.org/the-consequences-of-a-gluten-free-diet-craze/.

37. Jeffrey Kluger, "Eat More Gluten: The Diet Fad Must Die," *TIME*, June 23, 2014. time.com/2912311/eat-more-gluten-the-diet-fad-must-die/.

38. "Why Gwyneth Paltrow's Gluten-Free Diet Could Actually Be Bad for You," *Hits*, May 3, 2017. www.thehits.co.nz/spy/why-gwyneth-paltrows-gluten-free-diet-could-actually-be-bad-for-you/.

39. Lisa Schweitzer, "Wheat Belly Diet Review: What to Expect," WebMD, November 21, 2016. www.webmd.com/diet/a-z/wheat-belly-diet-review.

40. Rebecca, "Celiac Disease Is Not an Allergy," *Strength & Sunshine*, February 18, 2015. strengthandsunshine.com/celiac-disease-is-not-an-allergy/.

41. Jane Anderson, "What Is Gluten Ataxia?," Verywell, December 10, 2017. www.Verywell.com/what-is-gluten-ataxia-562400.

42. Quoted in Matt Wood, "Can Breastfeeding Prevent Celiac Disease?," *Science Life*, October 1, 2015. sciencelife.uchospitals.edu/2015/10/01/can-breastfeeding-prevent-celiac-disease/.

43. Quoted in Wood, "Can Breastfeeding Prevent Celiac Disease?"

44. Kristin, "Living with Celiac Disease (aka Going Gluten-Free When You Don't Want To)," *Iowa Girl Eats*, May 16, 2017. iowagirleats.com/2017/05/16/living-with-celiac-disease/.

45. "The Social Side of Living with Celiac Disease," Gluten Free Therapeutics, accessed on January 10, 2018. www.glutenfreetherapeutics.com/living-gluten-free/medicine-research/social-side-living-celiac-disease/.

Chapter Five:
Taking the Next Step

46. Katri Lindfors et al., "Future Treatment Strategies for Celiac Disease," *Expert Opinion on Therapeutic Targets*, vol. 16, no. 7 (2012): 665. doi.org/10.1517/14728222.2012.688808.

47. Quoted in "Are Enzymes Safe for the Celiac Disease Community? Researchers Set the Record Straight," Beyond Celiac, August 11, 2015. www.beyondceliac.org/research-news/are-enzymes-safe-celiac-disease-community-researchers-set-record-straight/.

48. "SVP for Immune Tolerance," Selecta Bioscience, accessed on January 29, 2018. selectabio.com/platform/svp-for-immune-tolerance/.

49. Kathiann Kowalski, "Silencing Genes—To Understand Them," *Science News for Students*, March 27, 2015. www.sciencenewsforstudents.org/article/silencing-genes-understand-them.

50. Quoted in Tricia Thompson, "The Truth About Leaky Gut," *Gluten Free Dietitian*, October 27, 2008. www.glutenfreedietitian.com/dietcom-blog-the-truth-about-leaky-gut/.

51. "Celiac Disease Treatment Licensed and Headed to Late-Stage Clinical Trials," *Allergic Living*, March 15, 2016. www.allergicliving.com/2016/03/15/celiac-disease-treatment-licensed-headed-to-late-stage-clinical-trials/.

52. Suesana, interview by author, January 31, 2018.

anemia: A condition where the blood lacks hemoglobin, or red blood cells, caused by iron deficiency.

antibody: An immune system protein produced by blood plasma that chemically combines with and neutralizes foreign particles in the body, such as bacteria or viruses.

antigen: A toxin or other foreign substance that induces an immune response in the body, especially the production of antibodies.

antihistamine: A drug that reduces the effects of histamine, a substance that causes the symptoms of an allergic reaction.

cytokine: A cell-signaling molecule that aids cell-to-cell communication in immune responses and stimulates the movement of cells toward sites of inflammation, infection, and trauma.

enzyme: Any of various complex proteins produced by living cells that bring about or speed up reactions (as in the digestion of food) without being permanently altered.

ferment: To undergo the process of fermentation, the chemical breakdown of a substance produced by an enzyme and often accompanied by the formation of a gas.

gastroenterologist: A specialist in gastroenterology, the study of the structure, functions, and diseases of digestive organs.

gastrointestinal tract: The part of the digestive system consisting of the stomach, small intestine, and large intestine; also known as the GI tract.

lymph node: A small, bean-shaped structure full of white blood cells that filters the lymphatic fluid and helps the body fight infection and disease.

peptide: A short chain of amino acids.

placebo effect: A beneficial effect in a patient following a particular treatment that arises from the patient's expectations concerning the treatment rather than from the treatment itself.

probiotic: A substance that stimulates the growth of microorganisms, especially those with beneficial properties.

trans fat: An unsaturated fatty acid of a type occurring in margarines and manufactured cooking oils as a result of being treated with hydrogen.

Beyond Celiac
PO Box 544
Ambler, PA 19002
(215) 325-1306
info@beyondceliac.org
www.beyondceliac.org
Previously known as the National Foundation for
Celiac Awareness, this nonprofit organization focuses
on improving diagnosis, advancing research, and
accelerating the discovery of new treatments and a cure
for celiac. It provides resources on living with celiac,
going gluten-free, gluten-free recipes, celiac disease
research, and celiac support groups.

Celiac Disease Foundation (CDF)
20350 Ventura Boulevard, Suite 240
Woodland Hills, CA 91364
(818) 716-1513
cdf@celiac.org
celiac.org
This nonprofit organization is dedicated to funding
medical research, education, and public policy initiatives
toward the improvement of life for celiac patients. It is a
good resource for information about celiac and NCGS,
finding a doctor who specializes in celiac disease, and
gluten-free meal plans.

Gluten Intolerance Group (GIG)
31214 124th Avenue SE
Auburn, WA 98092
(253) 833-6655
customerservice@gluten.net
www.gluten.net
This group aims to provide support for anyone living
with a form of gluten intolerance or sensitivity. It offers
publications for patients, a database of gluten-free
restaurants, and training for food service establishments.

National Celiac Association (NCA)
PO Box 600066
Newton, MA 02460
(617) 262-5422
managingdirector@nationalceliac.org
www.nationalceliac.org
An education and advocacy group for celiac patients,
NCA publishes the magazine *Gluten-Free Nation*
three times a year and an e-newsletter every month,
providing up-to-date information about celiac research
and the community.

University of Chicago Celiac Disease Center
5841 S. Maryland Avenue, Mail Code 4069
Chicago, IL 60637
(773) 702-7593
www.cureceliacdisease.org
This division of the University of Chicago Medicine
is dedicated to finding a cure for celiac disease. It
sponsors and conducts research projects and programs
such as Celiac Education Day, holds fund-raisers, and
encourages getting involved in the celiac community.

Books

Amidon Lüsted, Marcia. *Gluten-Free and Other Special Diets*. Minneapolis, MN: Core Library, 2016.
This book provides information and answers important questions about various popular diets, including the gluten-free diet, and includes recipes and activities to deepen understanding.

Centore, Michael. *Gluten*. Broomall, PA: Mason Crest, 2018.
Centore investigates gluten and how the gluten-free movement is changing the way people eat, as well as the medical conditions caused by gluten consumption.

Latchana Kenney, Karen. *Immune System*. Minneapolis, MN: Pogo Books, 2017.
The author introduces the structure and function of the immune system.

McAneney, Caitlin. *Gluten Intolerance*. New York, NY: PowerKids Press, 2015.
The author discusses the symptoms and dangers of gluten intolerance and the difference between gluten intolerance, celiac disease, and wheat allergies, as well as how gluten affects some people's bodies, how to avoid a negative reaction, and how to eat healthy.

Websites

Brainpop: Build a Digestive System
www.brainpop.com/games/buildabodydigestivesystem/
This interactive activity allows users to place the organs
of the digestive system in the correct spot in the body
and learn more about what each one does.

Celiac Disease Resource Center
celiacdisease.org
This website is a general resource for education about
celiac, the gluten-free diet, and gluten-free recipes.

Gluten-Free Living
www.glutenfreeliving.com
This magazine and web source is dedicated to the
gluten-free diet, lifestyle, and community.

Gluten Free Society
www.glutenfreesociety.org
This group educates doctors and patients about celiac
and NCGS.

Verywell
www.verywell.com
This website is a source for reliable, understandable
information on hundreds of health and wellness topics,
including celiac disease.

A

abdominal pain, 7, 19, 25
acid reflux, 47
ADHD and celiac disease, 24, 25
anemia, 19, 22, 59
antibodies, 14, 16, 20, 25, 26, 34, 45, 68, 78
   treatment targeting, 72, 75–78
anti-inflammatory diet, 52–53
anxiety, 19, 24, 39, 54, 64
autoimmune diseases, 6–7, 10, 11, 14, 16, 25, 29, 66, 76

B

bloating, 17, 22, 25, 60
blood tests, 16, 44, 50
brain fog, 25, 64, 65
breastfeeding, 68–70

C

celiac disease
   as autoimmune disease, 6–7, 10, 11, 14, 23, 35, 33, 59, 78
   diagnosing/testing for, 8, 11, 12, 15–16, 17, 20–21, 29, 77
   explained, 6–7, 14–15
   managing, 7, 21–22, 24, 43–57
   misdiagnosed/undiagnosed, 7, 8, 10–11, 12, 19, 23, 59
   moving forward, 83–85
   myths and misconceptions, 58–71, 83
   poorly responsive, 56
   refractory, 77
   research into cause, 28–49, 58
   research into treatments, 72–83
   risks if untreated, 59–60
   runs in families, 15, 21, 28–31
   statistics on, 10, 11, 15, 20, 24, 29, 30–31, 58
   symptoms, 6–7, 12, 17–20, 22–24, 25, 39, 64, 65
   types, 12–13, 19, 20–22
Celiac Disease Foundation, 19, 46, 50, 56
children and celiac disease, 22–25, 33–34, 39, 60
   failure to thrive, 22
   symptoms, 22–24

classical celiac disease, 13
constipation, 25, 47
cramping, abdominal, 17

D
depression, 12, 19, 24, 25, 39, 54, 64
dermatitis herpetiformis, 19, 20, 22, 67–68
diarrhea, 17, 22, 24–25, 47, 60
dietary supplements, 43, 49–52, 59, 75
dietician, talking to a, 46–48, 77
Different Blend Bakery, 50
digestive system, 7, 13–14, 17, 21
doctors
  directory of, 46
  seeing and following up with, 43–46

E
endoscopic biopsy, 16
enzymes, 47, 72, 73–75
  AN-PEP, 74–75
  inhibitors, 80–81
  KumaMax, 74
  latiglutenase, 74

F
fatigue, 19, 22, 25, 64
FODMAPs, 40–42
  cutting out, 55–57

G
gastrointestinal infections, 32–35
GBR 830, 76–78
genetics and celiac disease, 28–32
  gene inhibitors, 80
  HLA-DQ2 and HLA-DQ8 genes, 29, 31, 80
genetic testing, 16, 29, 30–32
gliadin, 14–15, 78, 80–81
gluten
  in the body, 13–15
  defined, 8
  misconception about, 63–66
  prevalence of in food, 10–11
  sensitivity to, 7, 11, 17, 24, 25–27, 40–42, 61, 63, 64, 66, 75, 84

ABOUT THE AUTHOR

Michelle Denton received her bachelor's degree in English and creative writing from Canisius College in 2016, graduating cum laude from the All-College Honors Program. She lives in Buffalo, New York, with her mother and two cats and has made writing her full-time career. She also works as props master and sometimes-stage manager at the Subversive Theatre Collective, and she is currently trying to find the time to write her first novel.